JUST ME
A·N·D·T·H·E
KIDS

A Course for Single Parents

by Patricia Brandt with Dave Jackson

Patricia Brandt is a single parent by choice, having adopted two children: Matthew, 12, and Renee, 5. Brandt is an associate professor in the Department of Psychology at Azusa Pacific University. Her academic focus has been in the area of human development and family life education. She also holds a marriage, family, and child counseling license in California. Prior to joining the faculty at Azusa, she spent eight years in Christian education and family ministry.

Dave Jackson and his wife, Neta, are the Editors of Marriage and Family Products for David C. Cook Publishing Co. Separately and together they have written several books. They have two children: Julian, 15, and Rachel, 9. Jackson also serves as one of the pastors of Reba Place Church in Evanston, Illinois, where he has been involved for ten years in ministry to families, many of them single-parent families.

JUST ME AND THE KIDS, A COURSE FOR SINGLE PARENTS
©1985 Patricia Brandt with Dave Jackson

Fourth Printing July, 1988

Scripture quotations, unless otherwise noted, are from the *Holy Bible: New International Version.* ©1978 by the New York International Bible Society. Used by permission of Zondervan Bible Publishers.

Published by David C. Cook Publishing Co.
850 N. Grove Ave., Elgin, IL 60120. Cable address: DCCOOK
Design: Gregory Eaton Clark
Cover: Barbara Sheperd
Edited by: Dave and Neta Jackson
Printed in the United States of America
Library of Congress Catalog Number: 84-71535
ISBN: 0-89191-750-0

Table of Contents

Introduction

Single parents may feel that it is "just me and the kids" against the whole world. And when things aren't going so well with the kids, the single parent may feel utterly alone.

The purpose of this course is to provide resources, build support networks in the church family, and offer training in some of the unique tasks of the single parent. All of it is designed to help the single parent move beyond that overwhelming condition of facing the world alone.

PART OF A SERIES

This course is part of a series of courses designed to minister to families in different stages of the family life cycle. Newly married couples have a great deal in common as they establish their new life together. They may marry in their twenties or thirties, but most of their tasks are the same. The same is true for parents of their first child, later when that child reaches teenage, finally when the last child leaves home, and when retirement is begun.

The situation of the single parent is not exactly a stage in life. But there are enough factors that all single parents share in common, that it is worthy of a specific course.

Some single parents, after taking this course, may wish to take whichever other course is related to his or her life-cycle stage.

The design for this series comes from the work of Dr. Dennis B. Guernsey in his book, *A New Design for Family Ministry* (David C. Cook Publishing Co., 1982). Guernsey, who is associate professor of Marriage and Family Ministries and director of the Institute for Marriage and Family Ministries, Fuller Theological Seminary, says that the family has critical tasks to accomplish in order to nurture healthy Christians.

Many churches spend the majority of their time and effort in remedial work—evangelizing and discipling people from families which in some past generation were thoroughly Christian, but failed to pass on the faith. Guernsey thinks we can avoid that tragedy by seeing our families as the church's most essential units and even creating "families" for those without. When the church becomes a healthy, ministering family of families, each generation will build on the one which has gone before, and more time will be released for reaching totally new people for the Lord.

WHO CAN TEACH?

With this perspective, the most effective teachers for this course and the others in the series are those parents who have successfully gone through a stage. They become the helpers to guide those who are just entering the stage.

So, if you are a single parent, and have "survived" for a few years, and if your children are doing reasonably well, you are the ideal teacher. You don't have to be an expert, and you don't have to be the perfect parent. All you need to have done is make it through some of the rough times. You can help others. This course will be your tool.

WHO SHOULD ATTEND?

This course is designed for single parents. It will be most helpful to those who have recently become single parents. But those who have been single parents for some time will be able to learn from others as well as pass on their knowledge and experience. Most important will be the relationships that can be developed between single parents.

HOW TO TEACH THE COURSE

This course can be taught as a Sunday school elective for one quarter, in week-night sessions (possibly in the comfort of someone's home), or as a retreat. Depending on the format you select, be sure to allow enough time for each session—at least one full hour. If that is not possible, consciously decide where you will shorten each session. Don't get caught running out of time at the end of each class or you might be eliminating the most important elements.

Your preparation for each session should begin by completing the *Advance Preparation*. However, after studying the rest of the session and before you try to teach the class, go back and review the Advance Preparation. Do you have everything that will be required? Have you torn the *Transparencies* out of the lesson book? Have you made sufficient copies of the *Resource Sheets?* Are there any special arrangements that should be made before class?

Each lesson begins with a stated *Session Aim.* It is a concise statement of the purpose or theme of the session. Later in the lesson, you will notice that each step begins with an *Objective.* It is specific and measurable. It tells you what you must accomplish in that step. Later, after you have taught the session, you can go back and evaluate yourself by asking whether you helped your students achieve each step's objective.

The *Steps* in each session are accompanied by the estimated time they will take. In the first session or two, evaluate how your teaching style matches those figures. If you consistently go over, then plan where you will cut back.

For your convenience, the portions of each lesson that you should be *saying to your students* are printed in **boldface type.** However, it is preferable to translate these ideas into your own words.

USE OF TRANSPARENCIES

The transparencies are perforated for easy removal from this book. Hold the book binding firmly with one hand, grasp the transparency with the other hand, and pull gently from the top to the bottom. If you have slight curling at the edges of the transparency, a transparency frame may be used to hold each transparency flat on the projector. After use, replace the transparencies in this book for protection during storage. This also makes them easy to find the next time you wish to use them.

USE OF RESOURCE SHEETS

Photocopy the resource sheets. If you cut them from the Leader's Guide, be careful not to lose the master sheets since you will need to copy the information on both sides.

By following these guidelines, you will find that you don't need to be an expert in order to teach a helpful, top-quality course to the parents of teens in your church.

Scheduling Your Resources

Session	Transparencies		Resource Sheets	
1			Course Overview	RS-1
			Negative Labels	RS-2
2	Self-Identity	TR-1	Building Self-Esteem	RS-3
	The Identity-Building Cycle	TR-2		
3	The Loss and Healing Cycle	TR-3	Behavior Matching	RS-4
			Finding My Place in the	
			Loss and Healing Cycle	RS-5
4			Self-Growth Contract	RS-6
5	When to Seek		Loss Roleplay	RS-7
	Professional Help	TR-4	Responses to Loss	RS-8
6	Facilitative Messages	TR-5		
7	Servants of Christ	TR-6	What Is the Function?	RS-9
8	Parenting		Your Energy Bank	RS-10
	Compensation Process	TR-7		
9			Building Trust Bonds	RS-11
10			Stages and Tasks	RS-12, RS-13
			Next Steps	RS-14
11	Three Components of		Real Men/Real Women	
	Self-Esteem	TR-8	Don't . . .	RS-15
	What Are the Differences?	TR-9	What I Can Do Best	RS-16
12				
13	The Aid Exchange	TR-10	Case Studies	RS-17
			Ephesians 4—	
			Order and Organization	RS-18

Who Are the Single Parents?

Session Aim: To become acquainted with this course and others participating in it. To discover the variety in types of single-parent families. To confront and dispel negative labels from others and from within ourselves.

Advance Preparation

For this session you will need to arrange various work spaces for the class—preferably tables around which three people can work.

It should also be possible for the class to regroup in a gathered seating arrangement.

Before class, you should make a collage designed to introduce you and your family to the participants. It will be important that this collage is simple (as an example of what others are to do) and viewable from a distance. See Step 1 for directions for making the collage.

You will need the following supplies for this session:

1. Collage-making supplies—large sheets of white paper, colored construction paper, glue sticks, scissors, *precut* magazine pictures and words, marking pens, and masking tape (or a means of posting the collages on the wall).
2. A chalkboard and chalk *or* a blank overhead transparency.
3. An overhead projector and transparency pen.
4. The course sheets, "Course Overview" (RS-1—be sure to fill in the dates for all the sessions before reproducing this sheet), and "Negative Labels" (RS-2). Make enough copies of the masters so that each participant can have a copy.
5. At *each* session be sure to have extra Bibles and pens or pencils for those who may fail to bring them.
6. In consultation with your pastor, create a poster titled, "Additional Help." List on it the names, addresses of qualified and approved counselors

and other helping agencies that might assist single parents. Post this in a prominent place throughout the course.

STEP 1

Introductions (25 minutes)

Objective: To give the class participants an idea of what will be covered in the course with the dates and times of each session. To introduce yourself to the class and help the class members to get to know one another in a way which will demonstrate the variety of families which are encompassed in the name "single-parent family."

After welcoming the parents to the course, pass out the sheet, "Course Overview" (RS-1) and briefly review the course noting the dates for the subsequent sessions. Draw the single parents' attention to the poster "Additional Help," and encourage them to contact and use the resources listed on it. Also, encourage the class members to bring to each session a notebook, Bible, pen or pencil and the resource sheets from previous sessions. (Allow no more than five minutes for this presentation and questions.)

Then ask the class to divide into groups of three and move to the prearranged work areas around the room. Encourage folks to gather with people they know least. (If there is an extra person, make two groups of two instead of one group of four.)

Write the following questions on the chalkboard or an overhead transparency, and have each person take a section of their large sheet of paper and make a collage answering the questions in a way which represents his or her household. Each parent should put his or her family name in large letters by the illustration.

1. **What is the makeup of your household? Who lives with you?**
2. **What life experience brings the most joy to your task of parenting?**
3. **What family experience or situation is most difficult for you?**

Encourage the participants to consult with their partners for ideas to represent their families. This will help them to get better acquainted. Be sure to stress the importance of keeping each collage simple. Time will be saved if you have provided precut magazine pictures and words or at least torn-out pages so that the parents will not become distracted by reading articles, etc.

While the groups prepare their collages, circulate around the classroom sharing with and encouraging the parents. Use this opportunity to begin getting better acquainted with each parent, family situation, and special concern.

Do not exceed the time limit for this step, but conclude the exercise even if some parents are not finished with their illustration. Have parents tape their collages to the wall around the room. As this is being done, summarize some of the variations, qualities, and issues which appear on the posters and encourage everyone to take a closer look after class.

Have everyone return to their seats for the next step.

STEP 2

Exploring the Issues (20 minutes)

Objective: To help the class identify the negative labels which are often attached to single parenting.

Lecture the following:

America has the highest divorce rate in the world. But divorce is not the only way that single-parent households are produced. Illness and death, prolonged business away from home, separation, adoption by singles, choosing to raise a child born outside of a marriage relationship—each of these also contributes to an increasing number of children living in one-parent families. In fact, the number of children in the United States living in single-parent homes has risen 60 per cent in the last decade.

Despite these increases, the single-parent family faces the additional handicap of having to function in an environment of negative labels.

At best, the single-parent family is usually considered "broken"—perhaps deviant, unstable, and abnormal. At worst, the one-parent family is labeled outright pathological (sick).

Americans have in mind the norm of the traditional family—one husband, one wife, and the children of this first and only marriage. And that is the ideal, but statistics show that less than 50 percent of American families fulfill this expectation. By the time of graduation from high school, fully half of all children will have lived for at least some period of time in a single-parent household. Real life, in its struggles, just as in its joys, often defies the ideal.

One single father said that the toughest label for him was the simple fact that he was "divorced." "I didn't have a script for divorce. Being raised in a Christian home with my father a minister, I was programmed for twenty-fifth and fiftieth wedding anniversaries. I could have handled those nicely. But having to say that I was an 'ex-father' or a 'divorced man'

held a lot of stigma for me."

A single mother said that "failure" was the label that hung over her most heavily. She said that once a friend asked her, "Who was wrong, who sinned in your marriage?" She was so shocked that she nearly fell out of her chair, but after she recovered, she could only say that she didn't know.

A widow said that even though there was no fault attached to her situation, she still had to be careful in company with other couples. She just wasn't a couple anymore and had to be careful that the wrong connotation was not put on her if she joked or was naturally friendly with men. She feared being tagged as a "fast woman."

Put these three labels (divorced, failure, fast woman) on the chalkboard, and invite the class members to mention other labels that are commonly associated with single parents. If the class has trouble coming up with ideas, the following might be suggestions:

> shattered
> sex-starved
> hard-to-get-along-with
> needy
> incompetent

Then review the labels asking the class members to indicate by raising their hands which of the labels they have identified with at some time. Write the number beside each label.

STEP 3

Thinking Is Becoming (15 minutes)

Objective: To help parents apply new insights by realizing the effect of negative labels on them.

Lecture the following:

It is important to realize that labels—both negative and positive—shape our feelings about ourselves and ultimately our behavior. The familiar Old Testament passages in Proverbs 23:7, "For as he thinketh in his heart, so is he" (KJV), reminds us of modern psychologists. They might paraphrase: "As one labels oneself, that is what one becomes."

There are lots of negative labels floating around about how bad it is to raise children in a single-parent family. We can't easily help what society tells us, but the real damage

occurs when we internalize those messages and tell them to ourselves. Our efforts must be to channel *our* thoughts in more positive directions.

The fourth chapter of Philippians provides some powerful advice in this regard. In verse 8 we are told to let our minds *dwell* upon excellence. To dwell means to focus our attention upon what we wish to become. Paul is speaking of spiritual maturity, but the same principle works in the practical matters of the home.

Consider the scenario: Lost shoes as the school bus approaches, and the car won't start making the fifth late day to work this week; last minute homework as the clock creeps toward 11, and tomorrow's potentially clean clothing remains piled by the washer; late child-support checks when grocery money is already stretched, and the lost shoes were never found making new ones mandatory!

Sound familiar?

Probably so. However, dwelling on positive, effective responses to family issues may be an important key to overcoming the negative labels which can loom over us when times are tough. Some parents might even find it effective to actually *visualize* themselves handling those sticky situations of single parenthood with an exciting self-confidence.

To focus our thoughts, to dwell, is also to pray. But keep in mind that Paul continues in verse 9 and expands upon his advice. He adds that we *practice* these things: "Whatever you have learned or received or heard from me, or seen in me—put it into practice. And the God of peace will be with you."

Pass out the resource sheet, "Negative Labels" (RS-2), and have the parents begin working on it.

In Column A write down sticky parenting situations—a situation which seems overwhelming to you. Then in Column B list your most common, present response to that situation. In Column C put the label you associate with yourself because of your response. In Column D try to identify where you got that label. Is it one you really believe, or have you just picked it up as a stereotype? Column E asks for an alternative, more effective response. If you are able to accomplish the new response, put the accompanying positive label in Column F.

Allow the parents as much time as remains to begin work on this sheet. Then close in prayer, encouraging them to complete the sheet before the next session. They should bring it to the next class session, as it will be used there in an exercise.

Life Without Fantasy

2

Session Aim: To help the single parent learn self-acceptance and acceptance of life's present situation. To rebuild an adequate and positive self-identity through a process of self-knowledge, self-disclosure, feedback, and self-acceptance.

Advance Preparation

For this session you will need the following:

1. An overhead projector and transparency pen.
2. The transparency resources, "Self-Identity" (TR-1) and "The Identity-Building Cycle" (TR-2).
3. On a blank transparency copy the questions in Step 3 for use in class.
4. Have extra copies of the course sheet, "Negative Labels" (RS-2), for those who are new this week and for class members who did not bring their

copy from last week. Also, prepare copies of "Building Self-Esteem" (RS-3).
6. A large newsprint pad, an easel to put it on, and colored markers to create a class notebook. Prepare this ahead of class with the title: "Parenting Joys and Struggles." Then list two or three *Joys* of parenting (in one color) and two or three *Struggles* of parenting (in a contrasting color). Use as your source items noted on various collages last week.

STEP 1

Beginning a Class Notebook (20 minutes)

Objective: To introduce and begin use of a class notebook—a diary of corporate prayer and praise.

Welcome the parents to the session and review some of the varied backgrounds and households represented by class members. (This was discovered in the collage exercise of Session 1.)

Introduce the class notebook of "Parenting Joys and Struggles" which you have prepared ahead of time. Explain that the notebook will be kept throughout the course in a location allowing for easy access by class members before and after class. Encourage them to add to it on a regular basis so that it will become a diary of class prayer and praise. They should list joys in one color and struggles in another color.

Invite the single parents to contribute some additional joys and struggles, particularly from this week's experience. Take only a few moments.

Read again Philippians 4:8, 9, and then spend time in prayer. Encourage several people to offer brief sentence prayers of praise to God for His faithfulness, even in times of difficulty.

STEP 2

Identity Development (20 minutes)

Objective: *To describe some of the components of our self-identity and explain how it develops and changes.*

Display the transparency, "Self-Identity" (TR-1), to demonstrate labels as a major source of self-identity.

Lecture the following:

Our self-identity is the picture we have of ourselves as we look at the many different facets of our lives. One could even say that our self-identity is the combination of the labels we attach to ourselves.

We have labels for ourselves as we function *spiritually, physically, socially, occupationally*, as a *sexual* being, as a *parent*, and even as we functioned as a *child*. (Point to the corresponding petals on the flower as you mention the various areas.) **Depending on your own experience, there may be other areas where you have labels effecting your identity.**

With a transparency pen add labeling examples in several categories. (The following example offers some suggestions.) Then ask the class to mention some of their own identity labels. Point out that labels and identity categories are not always neatly packaged. Overlap and inconsistency is normal. Also, note that some labels are more important than others.

Self-identity is formed early in life as we adopt what other people reflect to us about ourselves. Parents, family, teachers, the media, and other significant people in our life all have a part in shaping our identity. Even our life experiences and how we respond to them are a source of our identity. (Point to the sources of our labels illustrated by the soil out of which the flower grows.) **This is normal and natural. However, this is not the end of the identity story. We also shape our own identity through a process of risking and growing.**

Use the transparency, "The Identity-Building Cycle" (TR-2), and describe each of the steps in the cycle.

1. **The identity-building process begins with SELF-KNOWLEDGE. We gather information from many sources—as noted on the previous transparency.**
2. **Knowing something about ourselves and suspecting a corresponding label usually pushes us to reveal or test this information with someone else. Psychologists call this testing process, SELF-DISCLOSURE. We share a part of who we are in a wholesome manner when the sharing takes place within a caring relationship.**
3. **The FEEDBACK we receive in the self-disclosure step causes us to affirm, modify, or discard the label we were considering.**
4. **If the feedback confirmed a positive label or denied a negative label, we breathe a sigh of relief. But SELF-ACCEPTANCE can also come through confession and receiving God's forgiveness for our sins and failures.**
5. **In any case, self-acceptance yields GROWTH ENERGY. Of course, the more positive the feedback, the more vigorous the growth energy.**
6. **Then GROWING and CHANGE result as we step out with a new response to life situations.**

In this identity-building process new labels create new responses which in turn expand self-knowledge. And growth can continue.

Ask each class member to find a partner to work with over the next few minutes. Together these teams should review their homework from last week: "Negative Labels" (RS-2). Provide extra copies for those who do not have these sheets from last week.

You may need to review the concepts and categories to get discussions started. Circulate between the groups, helping the parents clarify sticky parenting situations, responses, and labels. Allow about 10 minutes.

STEP 3

Put on the New Self (10 minutes)

Objective: To help single parents discover a Scriptural base for a positive self-identity.

Have the parents continue to work in teams of two. Read aloud Psalm 139:1-6, 13-16, 23-24, and suggest that they shut their eyes and focus upon the words and images presented by David as he affirmed his identity before God.

After the reading, display the transparency on which you have written the following questions, and ask the class members to think about and discuss them with their partners.

1. **In a word or two describe what God knows about you.**
2. **How are *you* fearfully and wonderfully made? What are your wonderful works (i.e., your skills, interests, characteristics, labels, and roles)?**
3. **Where do you think God is leading you in the next year? . . . in the next five years?**
4. **In what ways might your identity labels be contributing to or hindering what God desires for you?**
5. **Are you allowing the Identity-Building Cycle to flow and grow? At what steps are you most likely to get stuck? When was the last time you experienced forgiveness?**
6. **Which parts of your identity enhance you? Which drain your energy and self-esteem? Upon which do you focus most?**

STEP 4

Enhancing Self-Esteem (10 minutes)

Objective: To help single parents indentify ways of building a more positive self-esteem.

Have the class regroup, and then lecture the following:

If our self-identity is made up of the various labels we see for ourselves, then our self-esteem is how much *value* we place on ourselves. It is the bottom line, the sum of the labels and how we feel about them. Enhancing self-esteem is a process of changing self-labels. Three commitments are key to this change process.

- **First, we need to recognize that esteem building is a process—a lifelong process which happens best with a knowledge of God's love and forgiveness to us. Beyond the basic foundation, the process grows through a series of small steps—most forward and a few backwards. But they always contribute toward expanding our life experience.**
- **Second, we must risk new experiences. Lives open to exploration and adventure allow God to shape them. We are like ships; God can only steer us when there is some forward motion. Moving the rudder will have no effect on a stationary ship.**
- **Third, we must be willing to share ourselves, our feelings, our victories, and our defeats with at least one other person in a warm and affirming relationship of mutual support.**

Reinforce these concepts by passing out copies of the resource sheet, "Building Self-Esteem" (RS-3). Suggest that the parents evaluate where they fall on the scales from one to five under each method of building esteem.

Close the session by praying that in the coming weeks each single parent will grow as God desires, especially in this area of self-esteem.

Loss and Separation, Anger and Guilt

3

Session Aim: To help single parents deal with the feelings of rejection, anger, and guilt that they may have experienced as a result of loss or separation. Whether one is a single parent through death or divorce or even through the experience of birth or adoption for a never-married parent, the emotional experience is often one of failure or rejection.

Advance Preparation

For this session you will need the following:

1. The transparency, "The Loss and Healing Cycle" (TR-3).
2. Copies for everyone of the resource sheets, "Behavior Match" (RS-4), and "Finding My Place in the Loss and Healing Cycle" (RS-5).

3. Chalkboard and five different colors of chalk or newsprint and five differently colored markers.

STEP 1

The Stages of Loss and Healing (35 minutes)

Objective: To help single parents understand the process of loss and the emotions which flow through the healing process.

Open the session with prayer, and then share the following:

When someone we dearly love dies, we expect to grieve. Some societies face the need for this more directly than others, and they have elaborate traditions for helping the bereaved person go through this process. Unfor-

tunately, our western society tends to rush or ignore people's need for this process.

Worse. We fail to realize that the same need for grieving accompanies other losses like the breakup of a marriage, the loss of a spouse and companion, and the loss of our identity as a married person. Even moving to a new neighborhood can trigger the same symptoms of a need to grieve that are evident when a loved one dies.

What are those symptoms?

One single father described his feelings at hearing his wife tell him that she didn't want him to come home anymore as a numbness. "This can't happen to me," he recalls. "But then there were the feelings of being rejected as I went through the ugly court battles to try to gain custody of the children.

"I never got to sit down and ask her why, so I never got out from under the feelings of guilt. I always wondered, wondered why? But I'll never know, I guess.

"After that came the anger. Sometimes I would just sit in my office for hours without accomplishing anything productive. It was so hard to admit that I was angry until I . . . to accept that it was okay to be angry.

"It was years before I reached the forgiveness and renewal stages.

"I remember one day watching a young couple walking arm in arm and thinking that that would never be my experience again. But a few months later I began developing some friendships with people who could listen to me, and I could listen to their problems. I suppose it was finding those new relationships and the therapy of talking it out with other people that brought me out of the depression."

Another single parent described her experience this way: "It started even before the divorce for me. I can remember it like dark waves of I don't know what coming over me. I did consider suicide, and that was very frightening. I reached out to a friend that called me long distance almost everyday to pray for me."

What are the symptoms mentioned in these experiences?

List the following on the board and then invite a few class members to describe their experience of loss and the impact it had on them. Briefly add their descriptions to the list.

    Numbness
    Rejection
    Bewilderment
    Anger
    No productivity
    Dark waves of dispair
    Thoughts of suicide

After you have listed several comments, go over the list using four different colors of chalk or marking pen to circle each response according to the category in which it falls: denial, anger/bargaining, depression, acceptance.

Much of our understanding about the stages of loss and grief come from the research of Elisabeth Kubler-Ross. Using the transparency, "The Loss and Healing Cycle" (TR-3), go over and discuss each of the stages in the cycle. You may wish to lecture the following or just discuss it.

DENIAL: In denial the impact of the loss is muted; the full emotional impact is not felt. We may feel the death or separation/divorce is just a bad dream. In the case of divorce, we look for signs of reconciliation. We may seek out ways to maintain contact. This is a difficult period in which to work out custody and visitation issues since each contact can also renew hope in children and parents that the separation is just temporary. The stage generally lasts several weeks to several months. If the loss was due to death, there may be a great deal of initial "braveness." People may comment: "My, you're holding up so well." There may be periods when one doesn't really feel the loved one is gone. One may imagine hearing him or her in the next room, etc.

ANGER: In anger the loss brings out a bitterness and a sense of injustice. Deep and angry feelings spill over into other areas of life when one least expects it. We are angry with ex-spouses, our children, our friends, with ourselves, but especially with God. "How could He allow such suffering in the life of one faithful to Him?" In divorce we go through a period of seeing our ex-mate in the worst possible light. He or she has no good points at all during this period. We may also find that this hate alternates with a bargaining process. We may imagine that a new hairstyle, new clothes, new interests, even a little jealousy if we get involved with someone else—maybe one of these will bring our ex-spouse back to us. This anger and bargaining process often fills the remainder of the first year and perhaps several months of the next year.

DEPRESSION: Usually at some point in the second year after divorce or death, the full realization of the loss—and its permanence—strikes home. The true grieving process has begun. We now need the space for a full and complete mourning process. In depression we find our moods gloomy; we may sleep all the time or we may have trouble sleeping; we lack energy, and goals seem unimportant; we retreat from people—even

our own children; and on top of all this we pile guilt, guilt, guilt. Without some good support and strong personal coping skills, this stage can linger on for years. Counseling is sometimes useful in this stage, since full expression of the sorrow is the only real way to get through the depression.

ACCEPTANCE: This is the closing stage of the loss cycle. In it we may look backward with a sense of sorrow, but without wanting to undo events or rework issues. It is a time of refocusing. New goals are established and new energies are released. We are ready for life again. The total cycle has spent its course. At the end of this second year (approximately), we tentatively move out into the world—perhaps a new occupation, new classes, new friendships. The third year is a year of acceptance. At its end we often look back and realize that healing has taken place. The healing process may continue well into the fourth and fifth year, but the basic foundations have been set in place.

Pass out the resource sheet, "Behavior Match" (RS-4), and have each class member work individually as they review the stages of loss and separation. After five minutes go over the sheet with the whole class.

STEP 2

Finding Our Place in the Cycle (10 minutes)

Objective: To help the single parent identify his or her place in the loss and healing process and to envision next steps.

Distribute the resource sheet, "Finding My Place in the Loss and Healing Cycle" (RS-5). Ask each class member to circle the stage which fits them at the present time, and have them identify and list their typical behaviors in that stage. Allow approximately five minutes for this process.

Some may be resistant to identifying their cur-rent stage and responses; others may simply not know. Don't pressure them to complete the exercise. Continue with the work sheet by reviewing the suggestions in the Healing Helps section.

Underscore the idea that all stages are normal and natural. In fact, all stages are needed for true healing and for the release to refocus to take place. For example:

● *Denial* is a protective device. It dilutes the full reality while we muster our emotional forces to cope with the loss.

● *Anger* helps us to separate.

● *Depression* helps us to explore the full impact of the loss. It slows us down so that we can eventually let go of the pain of the loss without burying the memory and the influence of the lost relationship in our own lives and those of our children.

● *Acceptance* allows a special time when it is okay to explore new options without thinking that it is "high time that we settle down" again.

STEP 3

Mutual Prayer (15 minutes)

Objective: To help single parents affirm and support one another in the emotional pain which is part of this growth process and to identify and use spiritual resources for healing and growth.

Ask each class member to find a partner, and conclude the session with mutual sharing and prayer between these teams of two. Use yourself to even out the number if that is necessary since the exercise works most effectively with no more than two per group.

Explain and suggest this prayer process: The first person prays for issues which are upon his heart and mind. The second person simply listens. When the first person concludes, the second person prays for the needs of the first person and then for his own needs. The first person listens and then concludes the session by praying for the needs of the second person.

The Cinderella Story

4

Session Aim: To help single parents develop assertive life planning by accepting responsibility for their own growth toward competence.

Advance Preparation

The focus of this session is on sorting through feelings toward being independent. It is particularly designed to assist women who may be having special difficulty becoming head of their households. It is a responsibility that most have not sought or prepared for. Some women feel that it is downright unfeminine, and yet it must be embraced.

For this session you will need the following:

1. Copies for everyone of the resource sheet, "Self-Growth Contract" (RS-6).
2. Enough envelopes for everyone.

3. A package of pipe cleaners, one for each person. Get yellow ones if possible.
4. A chalkboard and several pieces of chalk or a large piece of white paper spread on a table or posted on the wall and several marking pens.

STEP 1

One Is a Lonely Number (25 minutes)

Objective: To help single parents explore their feelings surrounding their independent status and their role as head of household.

Share the following:

All of us from the time we were little children have been socialized to think of life—particularly family life—as something to be

done in pairs. Thus, we feel a mixture of emotions when faced with the prospect of being a single parent/head of household.

Our feelings range from bitterness and anger to fear and anxiety. For women especially, there is often the fear *of* success and competency. After all, isn't it risky to become too able to care for oneself? To be feminine is often thought of as needing to be cared for and protected. If these dependencies are gone, then what of the womanhood? If one does not need someone else, then maybe there won't *be* anyone else!

Much the same is true for many men. The thought of making it alone is not pleasant, not normal, not desirable.

And this is understandable. God did not intend family life to be handled by one parent alone. God said, "It is not good for man to be alone. I will make a helper suitable for him." And certainly the same is true for women, especially when their task is parenting.

For those who have been married, the loss of husband or wife is not merely the loss of the companionship and support of a mate. It is the loss of a role or position—the position of wife or husband. As such, it is the loss of a major part of one's self-identity and often a source of one's self-esteem. Thus, the prospect of building a life alone and a family life as a single adult brings out all sorts of feelings.

However, even though single parenthood is not the ideal, it is the reality for those of us in this class. And it is important to embrace it.

Pass envelopes and pipe cleaners to everyone in class. Then ask those who do not have a wedding ring on to make a simple facsimile from the pipe cleaner and put it on the ring finger of their left hand. Next have them retreat to a place where they can be as alone as possible. There they are to consider the ring on their hand and its meaning. Then they are to take their wedding rings off (the real ones as well as the symbolic ones) and seal them in their envelopes.

Then each person should write on the outside of the envelopes, "**The ring is off. I am single. That means I will now . . .** "

They should complete the sentence.

While the class members are thinking and experiencing their feelings alone, write the above unfinished statement on the chalkboard or large sheet of paper. When the people return, encourage as many as are able to share what they have realized by writing it on the board or sheet of paper.

Note that this exercise may be quite emotional for some members, and some may not be able to accept the personal responsibility for their own life as symbolized by letting the ring go. Be understanding of this possibility. It is an exercise at the acceptance level of the loss cycle, and some may not be ready yet.

Be alert if some could benefit from this important transaction as they face the emotional issues surrounding their singleness.

STEP 2

But God Is Able (10 minutes)

Objective: *To help the single parent discover Biblical guidelines for competence and set his or her own goals in competence.*

Share the following:

As we think of our situation as single parents we can rightly paraphrase I Corinthians 10:13 like this: "No situation has occurred to you except what is common to other people. And God is faithful; He will not let you be tried beyond what you can bear. But when you are feeling overwhelmed, He will provide a way for you to cope."

Sometimes our hesitation in embracing our singleness stems from the fear that we *shouldn't* be competent. Some women have come to think that they need to be helpless in order to maintain their femininity. This is a fantasy, of course. Yet it is one that runs as deep within us as the story of Cinderella. Some women wait patiently for the handsome prince to sweep them off their feet and provide for their every need. Actually, only the most insecure men (those threatened by a capable woman) are interested in that kind of woman.

Certainly the author of Proverbs 31 valued a capable woman.

In this trying time, maybe the way God intends for you to cope is to more fully embrace the reality of your singleness and improve your competence.

Invite the class to turn to Proverbs 31:10-31. Have someone read each verse aloud as the class discusses the qualities and skills mentioned in the verse. List them on the chalkboard or flip chart. They might include the following:

trustworthiness
honesty
work with hands—special skills
hard work
planning and management
buying
selling
investing
concern for the poor
attention to appearance
fear of the Lord

The interdependence that God intended between two parents when leading a family is not achieved by keeping both partners incompetent. Therefore, for the single parent to increase his or her competence does not deny God's ideal plan or our natures.

However, *knowing* that it is okay to increase one's competence and *feeling* secure enough about doing so may be two different things. Sometimes we need a plan to get from where we are to where we want to be.

STEP 3

Competence Development (10 minutes)

Objective: *To review three sample situations in which competence needs to be improved.*

Share the following in an attempt to stimulate discussion among the parents concerning what area of competence is lacking and what might be done to improve it.

Consider these situations and identify what skill the person needs to feel more at ease. Then suggest how that skill can be learned.

A. **Stan needs to go out and buy some clothing for his children, Bonnie and Stewart. He feels intimidated by sales personnel and is tempted to call his ex-wife for help.**

B. **Jane's car is acting up again. She dislikes taking it in for repairs since the service manager always strongly suggests several additional maintenance jobs that need to be done, and she usually gives in and then feels sorry later.**

C. **Ethel is discouraged with her job. The pay is low, and the work lacks challenge and responsibility. She would like to return to school to develop new skills, but each time she tries, the plan falls through.**

STEP 4

Choosing a Plan (15 minutes)

Objective: *To help single parents develop a plan for growth in personal competence.*

Pass out copies of the "Self-Growth Contract," (RS-6). Have the class divide into groups of two. Have the partners work together on the first part of the sheet where they will identify where they need growth.

Explain that the priorities they identify at the top of the page may or may not be areas needing growth. They are to be listed there simply to keep them in mind as *priorities.* Without this clarification it would be possible to pursue a goal which might interfere with a priority. For example, if one parent had a priority of putting an insecure child to bed each night because the child needed the personal attention, then it wouldn't be good to take an auto mechanics course which met three nights a week.

The remainder of the contract is self-explanatory, but encourage the parents to actually agree to be in contact with each other during the coming week.

Helping Children Understand Separation And Loss

Session Aim: To help parents guide their children through the normal responses to loss and grief in ways that will minimize the children's tendency to fear abandonment or assume responsibility and guilt for the family situation.

Advance Preparation

For this session you will need the following:

1. The transparency, "When to Seek Professional Help" (TR-4).
2. Copies for everyone of the resource sheets, "Loss Roleplays" (RS-7) and "Responses to Loss" (RS-8).
3. Before class, assign the roleplays to different class members for presentation in class. Give each one a copy of the sheet, "Loss Roleplays" (RS-7), with instructions on who should work together on which vignettes. If roleplaying the scenes would be too awkward for your group, ask different members to be prepared to read them aloud in class.

STEP 1

The Loss Cycle
(30 minutes)

Objective: To help single parents understand the process of loss in children.

Open the session by sharing the following:

For children, the reactions to loss and separation from those they love can be charted more simply than the pattern for adults. For adults the loss cycle falls into four or five distinct stages: denial, anger/bargaining, depression, and acceptance/rebuilding.

For children the phases are usually: protest, anger, and hope. However, the simplicity ends with the charting. Because the verbal skills of a child are not fully developed, they often express their experiences and emotions through their behavior. In other words, they act out their feelings—their emotional pain—in their day-to-day behavior.

As parents we must carefully observe and interpret this behavior in order to understand how the child is coping with a separation or loss of a family member.

Some of the class members are prepared to roleplay children in different behaviors. As they are doing so, try to indentify which stage of loss response they are in.

Proceed with the roleplays. Don't allow too much time to be spent on each individual one. *After all of them have been done*, pass out the resource sheet, "Loss Roleplays" (RS-7), to everyone.

As the class discusses the different roleplays, encourage them to identify the behaviors which express different phases of loss. Record the class members' observations on the chalkboard by dividing it into thirds labeling the first third, "Protest"; the second third, "Anger"; and the last third, "Hope."

When the observations have been recorded on the board, share the following explanations of each phase:

Protest

In this phase the child is dealing with the shock of the loss. Just as in the adult loss cycle the first reaction is to shut down emotionally and sometimes physically, children may do the same. They may become passive, cuddle with cherished blankets or stuffed animals, want to be held, or refuse to eat. All of this may alternate with an alarm or panic reaction. Loss heightens the child's sense of vulnerability.

As the child sees it, his very safety and well-being is at stake. Alarm reactions include protests at being put to bed and difficulty in going to sleep, separation anxiety, reluctance in going to school or in going to play with a friend. Physical problems such as rashes, allergies, bronchial infections are common.

Later in the protest phase the child may deny the loss, respond with hyperactivity, reject the very one who has been lost, search for the lost one, become excessively disorganized, or cling to a dream of a fairy-tale reunion.

(If some of these reactions were not recorded from the vignettes, allow time to add them to the lists on the board.)

Anger

In the anger phase, the child is facing and working through the deep hurt of the loss which had impacted his life. Again, he will tend to do his grief work through his behavior rather than through words. Anger is particularly difficult for children to express openly because it often leads to further trouble. Sometimes they are afraid of anger because of its intense power and potential destructiveness. The child imagines that his own fury may cause more loss, punishment, revenge, abandonment, or even death. Finally, a child may get the message—intended or otherwise—that anger and sadness are not permitted in the family.

Behaviorally, the child's anger may result in an increased number of "accidents" to himself, his toys, and those around him. He may bully and fight; he may resist; he may passively resist; he may argue and complain; he may continue to display hyperactive and disorganized behavior. He may also develop further physical symptoms such as vomiting, asthma, or severe headaches.

In contrast to these behaviors the child could also become the "perfect" child—compulsively adhering to all rules.

Of course, none of these symptoms alone are indicators of how the child is doing. Most children resist, argue, and complain sometimes and hopefully obey most of the time. But what is significant to the processing of loss is a marked change in the child's behavior or the child's functioning at one or the other ends of the behavior spectrum.

Hope

Although there were no specific examples of letting go in the roleplays, each vignette had within it the seeds for accepting the loss and rebuilding. After the anger, the child moves on to the good-bye process. In cases of gradual loss there is time to actually say good-bye. In cases of sudden or unresolved loss (death, abandonment, or difficult custody battles) the child must symbolically say good-bye.

This letting-go process may be in the form of a visit to old places; it may be a letter, tape, or drawing. It could be a photo album or even a drama replayed with dolls and toys. The saying good-bye step is essential to the loss cycle. Without it the child will not be free to say hello to new situations and relationships. This is the key to an attitude of hope.

STEP 2

Where Is Your Child?
(10 minutes)

Objective: To help single parents identify the special patterns that their own children use to cope with loss.

Distribute the resource sheet, "Responses to Loss" (RS-8), to each member of the class. Ask the participants to work on it alone, doing the portions relating to protest and anger. Allow about five minutes for this work. Use this time to circulate around the class assisting any members who are having difficulty identifying specific behaviors. Assure the class that identifying the behavior is the important task. Assigning the behavior to a particular phase is secondary.

STEP 3

Next Steps
(10 minutes)

Objective: To provide single parents some suggestions of ways they can encourage the healing process within their families.

The following suggestions are ways that might be helpful for parents to use in helping their children cope with loss.

Protest

● **Maintain familiar routines without denying the fact and sadness of the loss. Allow plenty of time to talk of the loss with the children, especially if they are old enough to verbalize their feelings.**

● **Provide cuddle materials—blankets, fuzzy clothing, stuffed animals; return to earlier nighttime routines such as stories, rocking, nightlights, and quiet music.**

● **Provide healthy snack foods instead of insisting on large meals. Return to the more reassuring foods of younger days such as applesauce, mashed potatoes, etc.**

● **Be firm at times of separation but only after providing the assurance of a regular and trusted caretaker. Tell the child of the sequence of things to follow so that he or she can anticipate your return. Provide an older child with a watch. With younger children leave a key or some other significant possession that you ask them to care for while you are gone. This will reassure them of your return. Always call your children if you are delayed.**

Anger

● **When the child expresses his sadness and anger verbally or physically, take time right then to listen. This is the time for adults to put all else aside and give priority attention to the child. This is true even if the child is involved in abusive behavior which you must also curtail.**

● **Use your own physical presence to reassure the child. This is a time for touching, holding, sitting close.**

● **Provide play experiences in which the child can rerun the loss experience as well as release his pent-up anger. Plenty of physical outlets are in order with structure and rechanneling provided for agressiveness which might otherwise come out in harmful ways.**

● **Plan simple lists and reminders for the disorganized or hyperactive child. Use words for children who can read and pictures for younger children.**

Hope

● **Plan for good-byes, but don't force them. Watch for the child's signals for readiness.**

● ***After* the grieving, encourage new outlets and interests. Maybe it is time for piano lessons, swimming instruction or a new bike.**

● **Help the child maintain old ties and memories without living in the past.**

● **Encourage the child to build new relationships but not as a replacement to the old lost ones.**

A further resource would be the book, *Helping Children Cope with Separation and Loss*, Claudia Jewett (Harvard: Harvard Common Press, $11.95).

Allow time to discuss the above suggestions, then assign the class members to complete the remainder of the resource sheet, "Responses to Loss" (RS-8), as homework. Each parent should plan and attempt to carry out one helping strategy per child in the next week.

STEP 4

When to Seek Help
(10 minutes)

Objective: To provide some concrete guidelines for parents for when their children need professional help dealing with processing loss.

One of the major concerns for all parents when their children are going through hard times is the question of when are their struggles within the bounds of what is normal and manageable given the circumstances and when does the family need professional help.

Use the transparency, "When to Seek Professional Help" (TR-4). Cover all but the first point as you project it on the screen. Go over each point, encouraging people to take notes on it and inviting discussion. With this resource you are wanting the class members to write the points down as an additional teaching aid, to help them remember more than if they merely heard the points or had them provided on a printed sheet.

When you have gone over each of the points, close the session with prayer.

Remaking Our World

6

Advance Preparation

For this session you will need the following:

1. The transparency resource, "Facilitative Messages" (RS-5).
2. Extra pens or pencils.
3. The class notebook, "Parenting Joys and Struggles,"
   and markers.

STEP 1

How Does It Feel to Feel Good? (30 minutes)

Objective: To review a past, affirming experience in
order to discover its components.

Open this class session by reviewing some of the
recent entries in the class notebook. Allow an opportunity for members to pray together regarding these
and any other concerns.

After the prayer, ask the class to remain quiet
with their eyes closed while they think of someone or
some experience which made them feel good emotionally this past week. Have them visualize the incident
as clearly as possible, reliving the good feelings.
Allow about three minutes of silence.

Then have the class divide into groups of three
or four people each, and ask them to share with each

other the experiences they just reviewed in their imagination. For about 15 minutes have them discuss:

- *How, where,* and *why* did the nourishing experience take place?
- *Specifically,* how did it make you feel good?
- *What* makes an encounter nourishing or affirming rather than routine or negative?

(You might want to put the above questions on the board.) Conclude this portion of the session by reuniting the class and sharing the following:

Affirmation comes to us in many ways. Sometimes it is in the little things in our day-to-day experience, and sometimes it is the result of the larger sweeps in our life.

One single parent found that the most affirming experience for her came in losing herself in ministry to others. Not more than a year after she was divorced, two of her sisters were diagnosed as having cancer. Her attention then turned toward their needs and their pain. One of them was pregnant, and her baby died. But by allowing the Lord to use her in ministering to them, she was affirmed that she wasn't a failure in everything. She could meet the needs of others and show love as a sister even though she couldn't show love as a wife.

"Friends were my first affirmative experience," said a single father. "And then they guided me to some books, and some of the reading I did was helpful to me. After that I wrestled through whether as a Christian I could legitimately remarry again. I counseled with several people and received their encouragement until I could give myself permission.

"I also had to ask what I could, what should I do with the rest of my life. For me it has been writing and teaching. I enjoy both of those activities very much. They constitute finding myself again in tasks that are meaningful and challenging."

STEP 2

Two Components of Affirmation (10 minutes)

Objective: To understand two elements in communicating affirmation, and practice them in the classroom in preparation for doing them at home.

Share the following:

An affirming encounter may take place in a variety of settings and a number of ways. It can differ in its content in terms of words, and ideas. However, it will usually contain two foundational elements.

First, truly affirming experiences usually begin and are maintained by *Focused Attention.* Positioning the body in a direction facing the person to whom the affirmation is directed tells that person that he is noticed and important. Attention is directed toward him. Focused attention is also communicated through direct eye contact and perhaps even touch.

Second, *Facilitative Messages* contribute to an affirmation encounter. These messages encourage the communication process. The person receiving them feels deeply heard and understood as the other person nods his head in understanding, restates feelings or issues in ways which demonstrate understanding, or asks questions or requests further explanation rather than cutting the dialogue off. Facilitative messages use words that affirm and encourage.

It is important to understand that one can give focused attention and facilitative messages without necessarily agreeing with all the other person has said. This is a time for communicating understanding, not debating differences.

To reinforce these concepts, divide the class into groups of two, and have one partner spend about three minutes telling about an area of his or her life which currently lacks affirmation. Ask the other partner to practice focused attention and facilitative messages. Then have the teams exchange roles.

STEP 3

Strength Bombardment (20 minutes)

Objective: To help single parents design a plan for building self and family affirmation experiences.

Have the class members stay together in teams of two but turn toward you, and lecture the following:

In her book, *Self-Esteem: A Family Affair,* Jeanne Clarke explains that affirmation skills can include the use of rewards for simply *being.* We tell other people that they are lovable just the way that they are. Such messages are basic to the emotional nourishment process in our lives and in the lives of our children.

Another kind of affirmation is that which rewards what we accomplish. These are affirmations for *doing.* We need these rewards also to encourage and enhance self-esteem.

Both types of affirmation have a Scriptural base. Remember again Psalm 139, an affirmation from God of our being. Ephesians 2:19 is another: "Consequently, you are no longer foreigners and aliens, but fellow citizens with God's people and members of God's household." Yet in other passages we are called to be doers—to achieve, to accomplish (Jas. 1:22-24).

Because the single parent does not have another caring, observant adult in the home, affirmations for doing are sometimes missing. Though children may be appreciative of what their mother or father does, their immaturity prevents them from remembering to express it. So where does the single parent receive the deserved affirmations for doing?

One possible source, of course, is the understanding friends you are making in this class. But when that is not convenient, you can legitimately reward yourself with small accomplishment promises: "When the kitchen is cleaned, I am going to sit down for ten minutes and read my book" or "As soon as I meet my goal, I'm going to have an evening out with Mary to celebrate."

The only caution is that the reward be constructive and helpful. For instance, if you have trouble with overeating, you'd better not treat yourself with a dish of ice cream.

Display the transparency resource, "Facilitative Messages" (RS-5). Have the partners go over the points and then discuss a family member who is in need of affirmation in some area of his or her life. Have them brainstorm any unique ways facilitative messages could be communicated. Note the three components:

1. Messages which expand rather than constrict or cut off dialogue.

2. Messages which restate feelings and issues to reassure the other person that you are understanding.

3. Messages which affirm both being and doing.

When the participants have had time to brainstorm facilitative messages for one member of the family, ask them to copy down the categories on the transparency—questions that expand and not constrict, restatement of feelings and issues, and affirmation of both being and doing. As a homework assignment they should make a sheet for each family member on which they list a current way they might be able to affirm that person in each of the categories. Then they should make an occasion when they can try it during the week.

What Is a Family?

...7

Session Aim: To understand the family as a social and emotional unit having important Biblical functions rather than simply an organizational institution. The central emphasis will be on the building and maintaining of family identity and tradition within the context of the Biblical family function.

Advance Preparation

For this session you will need the following:

1. An overhead projector and transparency pen.
2. The transparency resource, "Servants of Christ" (TR-6).
3. Copies for everyone of the resource sheet, "What Is the Function?" (RS-9).
4. Extra Bibles for any who may have forgotten theirs.
5. Prepare six 3" x 5" cards with a family topic and prompting questions on each. (See Step 3.)

STEP 1

The Family Mobile (20 minutes)

Objective: To help single parents discover a Biblical *functional* rather than a **structural** approach to the family.

Open the session with prayer, and then lecture the following:

In her book, *What Is a Family*, Edith Schaeffer builds a model of the family out of the simple concept of a mobile. Each person has a part to play, and yet each part is separate. There is relatedness and nurture, support and

love, as the family acts and reacts together as a system. Yet there is also flexibility, independence, and a sense of separateness for each member.

The model is like that of the Body of Christ in Ephesians 4:16 where we are reminded that the whole body is "joined and held together by every supporting ligament, and grows and builds itself up in love, as each part does its work." We might even think of the family as a mini-church.

Traditionally it is difficult to see beyond a structural approach to the family—who fits into what role and who is supposed to do what. But a simple *structural* approach is not very helpful for the single-parent family because there aren't two parents to assign to different roles. However, another way to look at the family is a *functional* approach. The functional approach asks what functions or tasks should the family accomplish with all of its members.

Love and Nurture

When one looks for the functions that the family should accomplish, the Bible seems to indicate two broad categories. The first function of the family is to provide an atmosphere of love and nurture—a safe harbor, so to speak, from the tension and stress of the outside world. The family is to provide a sense of relatedness and care between each family member. Paul spells out this familial role of love and nurture:

"Therefore, as God's chosen people, holy and dearly loved, clothe yourself with compassion, kindness, humility, gentleness and patience. Bear with each other and forgive whatever grievance you may have against one another. Forgive as the Lord forgave you. And over all these virtues put on love, which binds them all together in perfect unity" (Col. 3:12-14).

Love, then, is the bond and mark of the Christian family. It is out of this sense of relatedness that family members learn to handle relationships. It is in the family that we learn to give and receive love, communicate needs, handle emotions, even grapple with the urge for power and position. In the family we learn to lead and follow. Here the foundation is laid for servanthood.

Order and Organization

The second function of the family is to provide order and organization. Peter clearly describes this function which provides rootedness and a sense of place and purpose.

"Finally, all of you, live in harmony with one another; be sympathetic, love as brothers, be compassionate and humble. Do not repay evil with evil or insult with insult, but with blessing, because to this you were called so that you may inherit a blessing" (I Pet. 3:8, 9).

The Christian family is to order its space, time, and energy as a model of excellence such that God will be glorified (I Pet. 2:12). In doing this the Christian family will also create a secure and predictable environment with which individual family members can identify, thereby enhancing the potential for their growth and development.

This sense of order and organization allows the family to socialize its members into specific life-style patterns—it reinforces family values. The final product is an independent, self-disciplined adult living out his or her values with freedom and conviction.

Use the transparency resource, "Servants of Christ" (TR-6), to illustrate two functions that the family should fulfill: LOVE AND NURTURE and ORDER AND ORGANIZATION. Invite the class to suggest additional tasks that might fit under each category and fill them in with a transparency pen.

STEP 2

Flexible Function or Fixed Format (20 minutes)

Objective: *To help single parents identify and list tasks the family is to accomplish through and for its members.*

Distribute the resource sheet, "What Is the Function?" (RS-9). Have the class divide into groups of twos and assign various teams different passages from RS-9 to look up. If each team has only three or four passages to find, there will be time to cover all the verses.

While the single parents are looking up the Scriptures, project the transparency resource, "Servants of Christ" (TR-6), again. It will help identify the tasks and functions that they are looking for.

Have each team fill in the Key/Summary Word identifying the function described in the passage. Then have them check whether it is a love and nurture function or an order-and-organization function. The sample below suggests what the findings might be.

	Key/Summary Word	Love and Nurture	Order and Organization
Proverbs 1: 8, 9	INSTRUCTION		✓
Proverbs 4: 1-4	INSTRUCTION		✓
Exodus 20: 12	HONOR	✓	
Deuteronomy 6: 1-7	VALUES		✓
Ephesians 6: 1-4	HONOR/CONSIDERATION	✓	
Psalm 103: 13	COMPASSION	✓	
Psalm 68: 3-6	CARING	✓	
Deuteronomy 24: 5	BRING HAPPINESS	✓	
1 Peter 3: 1-8	SUBMISSION CONSIDERATION		✓
Colossians 3: 18-21	ORDER		✓
Psalm 101: 1, 2	SERVICE		✓
1 John 4: 11, 12	LOVE	✓	

Allow about five minutes before asking the teams to share their findings with the whole group. Each team can fill in the findings of the other teams.

STEP 3

Building Family Traditions (20 minutes)

Objective: *To help single parent plan ways of building a sense of family for themselves and their children.*

Divide the class into six small groups with three or four people in each group. (If your class size does not allow for this, adjust your division accordingly.) Ask each group to prepare a short, one minute skit demonstrating a strategy that one of the families in the group uses to accomplish the family functions of Love and Nurture or Order and Organization. Give each group a card (which you prepared earlier) designating one of the following topics you want that group to work on and the focusing questions. Tell the groups that they will have only eight minutes to prepare their skit.

Love and Nurture

1. **Giving and Receiving Love**
   How do you tell family members they are loved? How do you encourage family members to show love to one another?

2. **Developing Communication Skills**
   What strategies do you use to encourage family members to "talk to one another"? How do you train family members to discuss their needs—whether these be physical, social, emotional, spiritual?

3. **Growing Emotionally**
   How are feelings handled in your family? What strategies do you use to encourage the expression and channeling of feelings? How do you celebrate happy events and remember sad ones?

4. **Handling Power**
   How do you train family members for independence and responsibility? How are decisions made in the family?

Order and Organization

1. **Socialization and Discipline**
   How do you train family members in the roles of life (i.e., student, employee, parent, child, male, female)? What special traditions do you use to help family members feel a part of the family?

2. **Christian Values Building**
   What values are important in the family? How can these be built into the lives of family members?

When the skits have been performed, close the class session with prayer.

32

Good-bye, Superparent

8

Session Aim: To free single parents from the notion that they must be all things to their children, compensating for the lack of two parents in the household by being the perfect single parent. To rebuild realistic parenting goals within the Biblical expectation of what a family should accomplish.

Advance Preparation

For this session you will need the following:

1. Copies of the response sheet, "Your Energy Bank" (RS-10), for each class member.
2. The transparency resources, "Parenting Compensation Process" (TR-7), and from last session, "Servants of Christ" (TR-6).
3. Have one 3" x 5" card available for each class member and extra pencils or pens for those who have none.

STEP 1

Perfect-Parent Message (20 minutes)

Objective: To help single parents identify "perfect parent" expectations that exist in their parenting goals.

Begin the session by sharing the following:

Every parent desires the best for his or her child. Every parent wants to be as good a parent as possible. As part of our self-identity, we carry with us messages about what good mothers and good fathers are supposed to be and do. Some of these are essential responsibilities, but sometimes these expectations are unrealistic.

We all have only so much energy. It is like

a bank account. Energy must be invested and saved before it can be withdrawn and spent. If we overdraw our resources, we will often run into trouble—too often that trouble will be in the form of delivering a bill of blame and frustration to our children.

Pass out copies of the resource sheet, "Your Energy Bank" (RS-10). Have the parents fill out the sheet by identifying how much each activity deposits in their energy bank and how much it takes out. They will find that some activities are almost entirely a drain—maybe that is true of enforcing rules. Whereas other activities such as having daily prayer may take a little investment to schedule and accomplish but return high yields in energy. Parents should indicate the energy drain *and* return for each activity by marking the scale from zero to three.

If a parent does not do certain things, like doing home maintenance, he or she might indicate the cost of getting someone else to do the job. If the task is outside their realm of experience, parents can rate it as two zeros.

An example would be as follows: Under "earning a living" a parent may indicate that it takes the maximum energy—debt=3. But there may be some important credits from the job because of the sense of affirmation for doing a job well. So one might score the credit columns as 1.

	"How much it takes out of me." Debit (−)				"How much I get out of doing it." (+) Credit			
	3	2	1	0	0	1	2	3
EARNING A LIVING	✓					✓		

Place the above example on the chalkboard or flip chart.

Encourage parents to work through the paper rather quickly without reflecting long on any activity. Their first response will probably be the most telling. Allow about five minutes.

Then tell the parents to count the number of check marks in each column and multiply the number by the value of the column. For instance, if one had six checks in debit column 3, the score would be 18.

Then combine the totals of all the debt columns and subtract that number from the combined total of all of the credit columns. This should result in a final balance for each parent's energy bank. Some parents may find themselves in the black, others may find themselves to be in the red—spending more energy than they receive.

Emphasize that this is not a precise tool in telling parents that they are overextended or have extra energy, but it will help them to think about their balance.

STEP 2

Perfect-Parent Patterns (15 minutes)

Objective: To help single parents identify patterns of compensation where they attempt to make up for the missing parent.

Project the transparency resource, "Parenting Compensation Process" (TR-7). Share the following:

There is often a compensation process that single parents participate in as they try to make up for the lack of two parents or the influence of the absent parent. These patterns include not only overindulgence in terms of material items such as toys, clothing, special excursions, or gifts, but also an overindulgence in terms of time. The single parent may feel that his own needs must always remain secondary to those of the children. But overindulgence in either the area of time or goods gives the child a false picture of life.

Another area where single parents feel like they must compensate is in balancing the overindulgences of the other parent. Maybe the other parent is a "sugar daddy" in terms of gifts. (A sugar daddy is an absentee parent who does not provide for the child's basic support but gives the child extravagant gifts that the custodial parent can't afford. The damage is in terms of the image of the custodial parent. The child may think that the sugar daddy cares more than the custodial parent who is actually providing the primary support for the child.)

The noncustodial parent may not provide the child with appropriate limits and discipline, so the custodial parent may try to compensate by overemphasizing those limits.

Encourage the parents to use a blank sheet of paper to list their children's names and identify ways in which they are "too tough" or "too tender" because of their efforts to compensate for the other parent. Have them fill out their sheets similar to the transparency.

Invite the single parents to share these insights with the class as they identify them. You can list them on the transparency, a chalkboard, or flip chart under the headings: "Too Tough" and "Too Tender." Sharing as they go may help some parents think of areas they would have otherwise missed.

STEP 3

Super Help for Not-So-Super Parents (10 minutes)

Objective: *To help parents who are feeling driven to be superparents or compensate for the impact of the absent parent by directing them to the Lord as their source of help.*

Building a new identity as a single parent is certainly not an easy task. It is made more difficult in Christian settings because of the pervasive feeling that a single parent family cannot successfully nurture and guide its children. Yet, while there are difficulties, single parents can provide with competence a warm Christian environment in which children can grow to maturity.

On the chalkboard or flip chart list the following Bible references:

Psalm 27:1-3
Psalm 46:1-11
Isaiah 40:28-31
II Corinthians 12:9, 10

Have volunteers read the passages, and then as a group discuss how the perspective of the Lord as our helper can relieve us of the compulsion to be a superparent.

Use the transparency, "Servants of Christ" (TR-6), from the last session to review the primary functions God intends for the family to fulfill for children.

God asks us as parents to provide "Love and Nurture" and an environment of "Order and Organization." These two functions should be our modest goals. To drive ourselves to do more is to court trouble.

STEP 4

Good-bye, Superparent (15 minutes)

Objective: *To point single parents to God as a way of releasing them from their superparent expectations.*

Conclude the session with a strength bombardment exercise. Distribute a 3" x 5" card to each class member. Ask the members to put their name on the card. Under their name they should state the area where they are most tempted to be a superparent or where they are most likely to try and compensate for the absent parent.

Then divide the class into groups of five or six people each. Have the people exchange cards among their own group so that each person has another person's card. Then allow time for prayer. They can pray aloud for the need of the person listed on the card.

Tell the single parents that when each need has been prayed for briefly, they should take a moment to write a blessing or encouragement on the back side of the card before returning it to the owner and dismissing their group. If time allows they might pass the card to several people in their group, each writing a blessing or an encouragement and the card gets returned to the owner.

Trust Bonds

9

Session Aim: To explore the nature of the trust bonds between parent and child, to be reassured of the strength of that bond but understand how it must change. Also some issues of the non-custodial parent will be explored.

Advance Preparation

For this session you will need the following:

1. Copies for everyone of the resource sheet, "Building Trust Bonds" (RS-11).
2. Before class ask someone to be ready to read Psalm 23 when you call upon them and another person to be ready to read Luke 15:11-24.

STEP 1

Some Ways the Trust Bond Is Tested (10 minutes)

Objective: To help single parents identify any anxiety they may have concerning the strength of the trust bond between them and their children.

Begin the session with prayer. Then ask the parents to show by raising their hands how many of them worry that the relationship they have with their children will be damaged when the child spends time with the noncustodial parent. Ask them to be more specific by responding to the following questions:

● **How many fear that the noncustodial parent will undermine the moral training of the children by instilling different values?**

- How many fear that the noncustodial parent plays the sugar daddy—giving the children fun times and expensive gifts in contrast to your ordinary discipline and unseen support maintenance? The other parent is fun and free while you are dull. What problems does this present for you?
- How many of you with older children fear that you are losing them, or that they will want to live with their other parent?
- How many of you have to cope with noncustodial parents who frequently let your children down by not following through with what they promise the kids? Do you feel the necessity to protect your children from these disappointments.

Allow a few minutes for the class to discuss these problems.

STEP 2

The Origin and Strength of the Trust Bond (15 minutes)

Objective: *To explain to the single parents some aspects of the origin and strength of the trust bond—what it is.*

Ask the people you have contacted before class to read the two passages: Psalm 23 and Luke 15:11-24. Then share the following:

These two passages express some important aspects of the trust bond, that bond that develops between a parent and a child at the very earliest ages. Without suggesting that Psalm 23 applies only to new Christians or that older Christians should leave the faith like the Prodigal Son left his father, let's look at the family.

Psychologists tell us that the trust bond between a parent and child begins very early—perhaps even before birth. This love relationship is essentially a molding of two individuals, the parent and child.

Separate bonds are established between each parent and each child in the family. One parent cannot substitute for or detract from the bond of the other.

In Psalm 23 we see the important elements of comfort, care, protection, and nurture. God is there when we need Him. God's rod and staff comfort us. With His rod or stout club the Shepherd beats off the foes of the sheep. With His staff He guides us through dark and dangerous places. When we are scratched, He anoints us with oil to bring healing and comfort.

It is when this same care is given to an infant by a parent that a trust bond develops.

The child can depend on the parent.

However, as the child grows, the bonds of trust develop a new dimension. So that the child will develop responsible maturity, the parent begins to allow the child to fail. If the fall is not dangerous and the stove is not too hot, the parent will allow the child to get a bump or feel the pain of too much heat when the child persists in going beyond the parent's advice.

So these are the two elements of the trust bond: (1) Nurturing and protecting the young child. But (2), when the child is older, the parent must have the courage to allow the child to fail. The trust bond is this two-way street.

The growth from one element into the other should be gradual. At first the child trusts the parent for everything. But slowly the parents begin to trust the child more and more. Finally, for the son or daughter to become an adult, the parent must release the child completely even if failure seems certain—just as the father did for the Prodigal Son.

One other very important aspect of the trust bond is seen in Luke 15. The father did not reject the repentant son after his failure. And that is a very important thing for parents. Failure must not be cause for rejection—whether the failure is small or large.

STEP 3

Applying the Concepts (20 minutes)

Objective: *To explore how these insights about the trust bond applies to the single-parent family.*

Share the following:

The question is often asked, "How can I, or even, should I try to be both mother and father to my child?"

Ask the class to respond in a brief discussion related to what has been said about the trust bond. Hear from several, and then point out that even though divorced, widowed, and adoptive single parents may sometimes feel as though they must be both parents, it is not possible.

If there ever was a genuine relationship to the other parent, it doesn't completely disappear and cannot be replaced. If this fact is ignored, serious emotional consequences can result.

The other side of this principle is the fact that the influence of the noncustodial parent cannot seriously threaten or replace the trust bonds you have with your child. (Though that doesn't mean your children won't try to manipulate you by comparing you or playing you off against their other parent. Such attempts aree normal.)

We have mentioned three applications for the trust bond:

1. **Once established, it is not easily threatened by external influences.**
2. **One parent cannot substitute for the trust bond that should exist with the other parent.**
3. **As children mature, the trust bond must adjust to release the children, allowing them to experience ever-increasing levels of responsibility for their own life.**

Have the class divide into groups of about four people each, and then pass out copies of the resource sheet, "Building Trust Bonds" (RS-11). Have the parents work on it together, discussing why they think one response is better at building trust than another.

STEP 4

Trust Bonds and Tomorrow (15 minutes)

Objective: *To help the single parents identify what is the next step in exercising the trust bond with each child.*

While the class is concluding the previous exercise, place the following on the chalkboard or flip chart.

Child's name/age	Next appropriate area of trust	I find release difficult because . . .	One smaller step I could try is . . .

When the class has finished the exercise from Step 3, reunite the class, and ask the parents to use a clean sheet of paper to copy what you have put on the chalkboard or flip chart.

Then tell them to fill it out for each child, dealing with one area of trust for each child before entering second and third areas.

After about ten minutes, close in prayer, asking that the Lord will give the parents wisdom as they try to take the appropriate next steps of trust.

Independence And Responsibility

10

Session Aim: To help single parents plan for the independence of their growing children and teach the children the skills of responsible behavior which will help them become independent.

Advance Preparation

For this session you will need the following:

1. Copies for everyone of the resource sheet, "Stages and Tasks" (RS-12 and RS-13, Cont.). This is a two-page resource. Make sure you have copies of both pages.

2. Enough copies of the resource sheet, "Next Steps" (RS-14), so that each parent can have one copy for *each* of his or her children.

3. Extra paper for anyone who may come without.

STEP 1

How Do Children Mature? (35 minutes)

Objective: To help single parents identify the independence tasks for children at each developmental stage.

Share the following:

Maturity is an interesting concept to contemplate. What exactly do we mean when we say someone is mature? For an adult, independence is certainly part of our ideal. We expect a mature person to manage the basic tasks of day-to-day living and be a responsible decision maker. We expect him or her to be able to hold a job, earn a living, and accomplish domestic tasks. If we dig a bit deeper we

may also find that we expect the mature person to be emotionally healthy and capable of initiating and sustaining intimate relationships.

We also expect a mature person to be sexually adjusted to his or her gender and accompanying role. Spiritual development is another part of maturity. We look for dedicated servanthood within the Body of Christ.

Such expectations are tall orders for any family to accomplish with its children. But in the single-parent family, fostering maturity can be particularly complex.

Let's identify some of the growing-up tasks which we need to encourage in our children as they get older.

Pass out copies of the combined resource sheet (two pages), "Stages and Tasks" (RS-12 and RS-13, Cont.). Have the class members divide into five groups according to the ages of their oldest child—infant, toddler, preschool, school age, adolescent. Do not create a sixth group for adult. (That stage is provided on the resource sheets as a sample.) However, if the groups are very uneven, you might ask some people to shift to a group which needs more people.

Ask each group to work on its developmental stage as identified on the resource sheet. They should attempt to fill in the tasks under the subheadings which correspond to the goal of that stage. They can use the adult stage at the end of the resource sheet as a sample.

When the groups have had about seven minutes to work, reconvene the large group and ask for a representative of each group to share the findings with the whole class.

They should report slowly enough so that those people who wish to may fill out the other stages on their resource sheets.

The following indicates the major tasks which should be included for each stage. You may wish to supplement the work of each small group by adding what they overlooked.

INFANT Goal: Trust
To develop security through physical comfort as physical needs are met in predictable patterns.

Physical	Social	Cognitive	Emotional
Crying	Attachment	Experimenting	Secure when
Grasping	Smiling	with cause	needs are met
Reaching	Babbling	and effect	
Holding	First Words	Mastering	
Sitting up		physical body	
Crawling			
First steps			

TODDLER Goal: Autonomy
To develop an I-can-do-it-myself confidence through increased mastery of physical skills.

Physical	Social	Cognitive	Emotional
Self-feeding	Parallel play	Language—concepts and	Freedom within boundaries
Dressing/	with others	two-word	Appropriate
Undressing	Says, "No"	sentences	choices
Running	Says, "I can	Very literal	
Climbing stairs	do it"	Distinguishes	
Throwing		between male	
Jumping		and female	
Toilet training		Rules external	
		Obedience tied	
		to negative	
		sanctions	

PRE-SCHOOL Goal: Initiative
To develop an increased sense of separateness through making independent choices and initiating activities based on personal preference.

Physical	Social	Cognitive	Emotional
Climbing	Attachment to	Language—lots	Freedom to initiate
Riding	same sex	of vocabulary,	within a clear
Hopping	beginning	whole	structure
Swinging	Loves opposite	sentences	
Simple chores	sex parent	Use of concepts	
like picking	Self-centered	expands	
up toys	play but	Fantasy and	
or clothes,	with other	pretending	
emptying trash,	children	Rules are external	
dusting, etc.		(rewards and	
		consequences)	
		Counting	

SCHOOL-AGE Goal: Industry
To develop the special skills and talents which increase competence at home, at school, at church, and in the neighborhood.

Physical	Social	Cognitive	Emotional
Skipping	Mutual sharing	Saving for	Feels competence
Jumping rope	play	special	based on
Throwing,	Attachment to	purpose	accomplishment
hitting a	same sex role	Academic skill	of skills
small ball	model	building	
Kicking	Hobbies, sports	Knowing and	
Art ability	Groups, clubs,	following rules	
Complex chores	best friends	Following	
like cooking,		instructions	
laundry, bed			
making, etc.			

ADOLESCENT Goal: Identity
To develop an integrated and independent sense of self, separate from family but related to friends.

Physical	Social	Cognitive	Emotional
Rapid bodily	Sharing in	Abstract and	Experimenting
growth	friendships	symbolic	with a variety of
Sexual maturity	Interest in	thought	roles from a
Pimples	opposite sex	Role taking	secure base
Independence	Dating	Ability to see	Frequent emo-
in household	Independent	another's	tional turmoil
chores	activities	point of view	as new things
	Leadership	Fantasy about	are explored
	Working outside	future goals	
	family	Money	
		management	

(Material for the adult stage is not included here since it is provided already on the resource sheets.)

STEP 2

The Unique Nature of Each Child (10 minutes)

Objective: To help single parents realize that even though there are natural tasks of maturity for each stage in a child's development, each child is different and will realize those tasks in a different style.

Share the following:

Even though there are natural tasks to accomplish in each stage of a child's development, each child is different and will therefore realize those tasks in different styles.

These differences are not simply matters of taste and interest. Different tastes and interests are legitimate and must be accounted for, but there are greater variations between people —even in the same family—which might be called life perspectives. Psychologist, Carl G. Jung, has been helpful in describing these for us.

Each person has a unique combination of temperament, physical make-up, energy level, thinking style, and problem solving strategies. These come together to produce a special life perspective. And that life perspective affects how the person perceives all that goes on around him or her, and it affects how the person responds to those stimuli.

Place the four style variable categories on the board as you share the following information about each variable.

Introversion ⟶ to ⟵ Extroversion

Each of these areas can be seen as a spectrum or a scale on which any person falls. The more introverted person draws energy from within himself. He enjoys activities and problem solving by himself.

The extroverted person is drained by too much time alone. He needs to be around other people. He enjoys group activities and problem-solves best with the help of others.

Thinking ⟵ to ⟵ Feeling

The thinker speculates about the issues and relationships of his life. He plans carefully and completely before entering into any new ventures or relationships. He evaluates everything.

The feeler goes by his gut! He empathizes strongly with the feelings and problems of those around him—sometimes too much. He is often overloaded emotionally and finds it difficult to plan completely before acting on a feeling.

Mechanical ⟵ to ⟷ Verbal

The mechanical person manages *things*, even communicates best with things. The mechanical person expresses love with material gifts and enjoys fully the physical pleasures of life.

The verbal person communicates with words and expresses love verbally. The talker enjoys nothing more than a deep and intimate time of verbal conversation. The strongly verbal person has a great deal of difficulty understanding the nonverbal, mechanical person. And the mechanical person can't understand what all the fuss is about.

Closed ⟶ to ⟷ Open

Closed and open are not qualities which can be labeled good or bad, healthy or unhealthy unless they occur in an extreme form. The closed person needs his ends tied up neatly. Careful adherence to routines and schedules is valued. Adventure is planned and then enjoyed.

The open family member, on the other hand, jumps eagerly and spontaneously into the adventures of life. Planning seems to take the spice out of life for him or her. Routines and schedules, if there are any, are changed frequently. Deadlines don't have much influence on the open individual.

(Notice here that we are not using the word "closed" to mean secretive or "open" to mean one who shares freely. We are speaking of closed or open responses to the unpredictable.)

In each of these areas there is not one way which is better than the other. You and your children will fall at different places on the scale from one side to the other. Insofar as it is possible, we should respect and flow with a person's style. Only when it tends toward the extreme of the spectrum on either end, is it necessary to urge the person to modify his or her approach in that area of life. Of course, in different settings, one approach may have a functional advantage over another. But the tables will turn in another setting.

Ask the class members to use a blank sheet of paper on which they create scales for each of the four variables. Then on each scale they should indicate where they and each of their children fall. Put the following example on the chalkboard or flip chart. Allow about three minutes for the parents to work.

Introversion $\longleftarrow$ Bill Mom Jerry $\longrightarrow$ Extroversion

STEP 3

Steps to Independence (15 minutes)

Objective: To help single parents plan one specific strategy for each child's next step in developing independence and responsibility—a step which is in harmony with their unique nature.

Pass out copies of the resource sheet, "Next Steps" (RS-14), so that each parent can have one copy for each of his or her children.

Ask the parents to follow along as you talk them through a sheet for one of their children.

After filling in the child's name, indicate the developmental stage that the child is in—infant, toddler, preschool, etc. Then get out your resource sheets, "Stages and Tasks" (RS-12 and RS-13, Cont.), and write down any tasks your child has mastered for his or her stage. For example, maybe school-age Bobby is good in sports, knows and follows rules pretty well, and has good academic skills.

Then under point four identify one task which should be worked on. Maybe our example,

Bobby, has trouble saving any of his money for special purposes.

Next, evaluate *this* task in terms of his life perspectives which you identified on the sheet earlier. Bobby, for example, may be rather extroverted and spends his money to buy candy for friends. So, in terms on the Introversion/Extroversion scale, saving money might rate a two, rather hard. But on the Mechanical/Verbal scale, maybe he was more mechanical—able to manage. That will help him in managing money. But that style also involves communicating with things, making it hard to control his giving candy, etc. On this scale you might mark a three, since the hard and easy parts balance out.

Under point six, list one small step to guide your child into independence and responsibility in this task area. Maybe for Bobby, it would be to get him to keep an accurate record of how he spends his money. (Before he can control his money, he must know what is happening to it.)

Step seven asks you to identify what you must do to get the growth under way. Maybe Bobby's parent needs to get Bobby a little note pad, and show him how to keep an account, then check up on him every three days to see that he is filling it out.

Have the class members take these sheets home and fill out and start on the tasks with their other children during the next week.

Sexual Identity In the Single-Parent Family

.11

Session Aim: To identify some of the aspects of a healthy sexual identity, and to identify some of the challenges the single parent faces in guiding children when there is only one sex-role model in the home. To devise a plan for how to meet these challenges and develop a healthy sexual identity in children.

Advance Preparation

For this session you will need the following:

1. Copies for everyone of the resource sheets, "Real Men/Women Don't . . ." (RS-15) and "What I Can Do Best" (RS-16).
2. The transparency resources, "Three Components of Self-Esteem" (TR-8) and "What Are the Differences?" (TR-9).

STEP 1

The Development of Sexual Identity (15 minutes)

Objective: To explain the development of sexual identity in the context of self-esteem. And to explain how parents contribute to the development of one's sexual identity.

Share the following:

"I don't want Bill to grow up to be a sissy," **one widowed mother recently said. "But how** **will he know how to be a man when there is no** **model in our home?"**

A divorcee also wondered, "How can my **daughters, growing up in a female household,** **learn what men are like?"**

These are natural questions for many

single parents. We want our children to be adjusted to their own sex, and we want them to know how to get along with the opposite sex. We usually expect these tasks to be accomplished in the home as children interact with two parents—a role model of each sex.

To understand how we as single parents can deal with these questions, it may be good for us to look first at the roots of a child's overall self-esteem.

Display the transparency, "Three Components of Self-Esteem" (TR-8). Refer to it as you lecture the following.

Let's visualize self-esteem as a three-legged stool. The legs might be labeled "sense of worth," "sense of adequacy," and "sense of identity."

The *sense-of-worth* leg represents how a child feels loved. And parents are the most significant persons in communicating this to a child.

Love includes several things which can all be adequately provided by the single parent. It is communicated through direct statements: "I love you." It should include warm hugs and kisses, affectionate touches, and special remembrances. Love is communicated through the cheerful provision of necessities. And Scripture tells us (particularly in Heb. 12) that love must also involve fair discipline.

A *sense of adequacy* is the feeling of competence, the confidence that "I can do it." This is developed in children as they explore the world and develop new skills. The parent's role must include monitoring the child's spirit. Does the child wonder about his own adequacy because he notices that others hesitate to challenge him? Or, have challenges which are too hard overwhelmed the child? These are the two extremes to avoid.

Dr. Dennis B. Guernsey, Director of the Institute for Marriage and Family Ministries at Fuller Theological Seminary, thinks the parent of the same sex as the child has the most to contribute to these feelings of competence. The father has the most responsibility for instilling within his son a sense of adequacy. And the mother will be most successful in communicating the same to her daughter.

The *sense of identity* is the child's certainty that he or she *belongs* and is *unique*—being a part of the family and yet especially unique. These two aspects of identity must be balanced.

A parent can help to create a sense of belonging for everyone in the family by together activities, inclusive words like "we," family traditions, and shared chores and shared decisions.

A child's uniqueness and specialness can be fostered by valuing what each child can contribute. Each child can develop a specialty. And care should be taken not to compare children negatively to siblings with comments like, "If you were only good like your big sister."

It is this leg of the stool that includes a child's sexual identity—confidence in the child concerning his or her own gender *and* an understanding of what that means behaviorally. At a young age a child should learn his or her gender with certainty. In this session we won't try to describe the process of how a child internalizes this fact, but it is a very important process that needs stable and consistent contacts with adults of both sexes.

However, once a child knows its gender, there is the ongoing discovery of what that means. Again there is a role for both fathers and mothers. When a boy is developing an image of what it means to be a man, he will most likely look to his father as a model. Similarly, when a girl is establishing what it means to be a woman, she will look to the example of her mother.

But a young child may have feelings of falling short of the maturity expressed by the adult model of the parent. Mother may provide her daughter with an excellent model of womanhood while at the same time creating tension over how far beyond the little girl she is. This is where the father's input is again critical.

According to Guernsey, sexual identity is most effectively *affirmed* by the opposite-sex parent. This is only logical: A father can most effectively assure his daughter that she is delightfully different or unique from him. And the mother underscores the same for her son as she reinforces her respect and value for his maleness.

The same-sex parent provides the model; the opposite-sex parent affirms progress toward that model.

There are two additional tasks that a father normally accomplishes in the two-parent family. He helps his son separate from the protective skirts of the mother in a way that encourages his adventuresome manhood. This separation also prepares him to be able to love another woman—his future wife. The task with the daughter is slightly different. The father is the first male she falls in love with. For her, these new and important feelings are the seeds for a fulfilling marriage. A good father both nurtures and then redirects them. Emotionally he communicates, "It's not me; I belong to your mother. But someday there will be a husband whom you can love and give yourself to fully."

Though these tasks may happen somewhat automatically in most two-parent families, even some two-parent families have difficulty reinforcing the sexual identity of their children if the parents do not understand these functions and work to fulfill them.

But what is a single parent to do when there is not an adult of each sex in the household? The wise single parent can compensate with careful planning. First, we must understand the importance for our children of regular contact with loving and trustworthy adults of both sexes. Second, we must concentrate on the aspects of the developmental process we can do best. Third, we must get help in the tasks we cannot perform.

In these ways we can be competent single parents.

The needs of our children to have ongoing contact with loving adults of both sexes are sometimes the most compelling reasons to maintain contact with the noncustodial parent.

STEP 2

The Importance of Sexual Identity (20 minutes)

Objective: To discover the relevance of a clear sexual identity for children, but to caution against reducing one's sexual identity to stereotypes.

Pass out the resource sheet, "Real Men/Women Don't . . ." (RS-16). Have the class divide into small groups of about four people each and work together on filling out the sheet. Recommend that they alternate between filling in something for men and then something for women.

Allow about six minutes for this exercise, then reconvene the large group and invite discussion or comments for about four minutes.

Whether this exercise met with a lot of agreement, vigorous disagreement, or stimulated a good laugh for everyone, will depend on the perspectives of your people. Share the following:

This exercise was not intended to establish what men and women should or should not do. Instead, it should point up how culturally based the differences between men and women are if the question is asked in terms of roles and tasks.

We are living in an age when many of the old stereotypes are breaking down. Whether you wish to preserve them or help change them, there are some important implications. The person who wishes to pass on the old expectations will lead his or her children into a world where there are few cultural supports. Will you have given your children a solid base for understanding the differences between men and women? Or will those notions crumble in the world of experience?

However, the person who wants to be a part of breaking down all the old stereotypes has a danger, too. Much of the effort to change expectations for what boys and girls can become—nurses or truck drivers, doctors or airline attendants—starts at the earliest years with degendering role expectations. That may be good in terms of careers, but you'd better ask what symbols you will give your children to reinforce their gender identity. The naive approach of some reformers has been to emphasize to children at the youngest years that there is no difference between males and females. There may be no difference in what each can do in terms of career, but that is quite distinct from suggesting that there is no difference. What are the differences?

Display the transparency, "What Are the Differences?" (TR-9).

In terms of what males and females can *do* distinct from each other, there aren't many differences. Men can, of course, be fathers, and women can be mothers. Because they have larger muscles, slight differences in bone structure, and a better oxygen delivery system, males tend to be stronger, faster, and more agile. Women are more flexible and may excel in certain endurance tests. Women seem to have slightly more tolerance for pain. They develop earlier, both physically and mentally. (This may have an effect on education and why boys and girls seem to excel in different subjects: Those subjects may be taught when the mind of one sex is more receptive than the other.) Males are more susceptible to some physical and emotional diseases than females. However, women seem to have more problems with depression than men. There are more females born and they live longer than males.

Other differences seem to differ greatly between individuals, though some tests suggest that females are more intuitive and verbal and some males are more spacially oriented and aggressive. But in many things culture plays a greater role than sex.

Greater than all these characteristics is the fact that every cell in a boy is distinctly male, and every cell in a girl is female. All cells in a female have two X chromosomes. Every cell in a male has one X and one Y chromosome.

Have someone in the class read Genesis 1:27, and take a few minutes to discuss the meaning of this verse in light of the other material which has been presented. Some things you might want to note are that by being created in the image of God, mankind as a whole has many qualities and abilities which are alike for men and women in reflecting our Creator. However, God did designate a distinction between males and females which must be recognized and honored.

STEP 3

Enhancing Sexual Identity (15 minutes)

Objective: To help single parents identify what ways they can best help their individual children with their sexual identity and to devise a plan to compensate for needs.

Have the class divide into groups of three people each. Encourage people who know each other well to group together. Pass out copies of the resource sheet, "What I Can Do Best" (RS-16). Encourage the parents to fill out the blanks in the center two columns by using complete sentences containing their child's name in the following fashion: "**In terms of sexual identity, I can help Johnny . . .**" and "**A person of the opposite sex is needed to help Johnny . . .**"

Then in the right-hand column have the parents list the names of two or three people of the appropriate sex who might be able to help. Possible candidates are the noncustodial parent, grandparents, aunts and uncles, scout leaders, persons in Big Brother/Big Sister or Indian Princess programs, concerned church members, and caring neighbors.

STEP 4

Putting the Plan to Work (10 minutes)

Objective: To give the single parents some suggestions for how they might put the plan into effect to gain more input from the adults of the opposite sex.

Ask the class to regroup, and then share the following:

Now that you have some suggestions for who might help your family in terms of sexual-

identity balance, it will be important to put the plan into practice. You may be tempted to think that your children will be adequately exposed to adults of the other sex as they naturally move into the broader community. That may be true if you are a man and your children need exposure to women. But if you are a woman, and your children need to interact with men, the chances for most children under junior high age of having a male teacher in school or Sunday school are often less than one in ten. It is better to be deliberate than to rely on chance.

When you approach the person or persons you are seeking help from, it may be helpful to tell them a little of the "why" for wanting to involve other adults in the lives of your children. The notes from this session will help. A person who doesn't know what he or she is supposed to do, won't be of much help unless that person instinctively knows what to do.

Caution should be noted concerning whom you seek help from. If you have any reservations about the trustworthiness of the person, listen to your intuition, and find someone else. It is unfortunate that it needs to be mentioned, but the statistics on sexual abuse of children are shocking. And relatives, baby-sitters, and family acquaintances are not necessarily safe.

If you are dating, it is probably unwise to expect the person you are dating to fulfill these needs for your children. It would load the relationship with too much baggage, and it might be too tenuous for your children.

Also, be careful to not let this arrangement with a helping adult involve you intimately in a way you are not wanting. It is a "family matter," and as such you and the other person may begin to feel like parents together. Take care that the relationship does not become adulterous.

Some safeguards for these problems are to involve a third person, work as parents together in a larger group, involve the noncustodial parent as much as possible, or seek help from an uncle or grandfather.

There are dangers, but the needs of our children can motivate us to find solutions which will safely give them what they need in the development of their sexual identity.

Close the session in prayer, asking the Lord to help the parents as they seek assistance in areas where they need it.

Outlets with The Kids and Without Them

12

Session Aim: To help single parents explore new social and emotional outlets involving children and adults as well as adults alone. The uneasiness which surrounds building a new social life alone and coping with sexual and intimate encounters will be considered.

Advance Preparation

For this session you will need the following:

1. Travel posters, travel and vacation brochures, pictures from magazines depicting family outings as well as pictures showing adult activities of a social or recreational nature. You may want to recruit help from several of the more active class members. Decorate the classroom with these items before the session.
2. Prepare or have someone else prepare coffee, tea, and other light snacks to be served before class.
3. Prepare a large poster to be displayed near the refreshments with the following questions:
   - What was your best family adventure?
   - What was your best adult adventure?
   - What would you like to do?
   - What's stopping you?

STEP 1

Adventures Ahead
(20 minutes)

Objective: To help single parents discover new social activities for the family as well as new social activities for adults.

As people come in, encourage them to gather around the coffee and refreshments as they think about and discuss the questions on the poster.

When most people have arrived and had a few minutes to visit, invite people to find seats and begin with prayer, thanking God for the adventure of life.

Then have everyone get out pencil and paper. Provide those supplies for any who may have come without. Ask the parents to write down their answers to the questions on the poster. Make them more specific this way:

● *What was your best family adventure?* **Answer this question in terms of your single-parent family. What activity or outing has been most enjoyable for you and all the kids?**
● *What was your best adult adventure?* **Again the time frame is since you have been a single parent. It doesn't have to be some great exploit. Just what has been most enjoyable to you?**
● *What would you like to do most?* **Answer this in two parts: as a family and as an adult alone. Don't list things that are financially unreasonable for you, but do list what you'd like to do if other hurdles could be overcome.**
What's stopping you? **Answer this in two parts, also: as a family and as an adult alone.**

Allow the class about five minutes to answer these questions. If the poster is not visible, move it to where all can see, or else write the questions on the board.

After the questions have been answered, have as many class members share their answers as possible. Encourage all who are listening to write down any ideas they hear that they might like to try. The purpose is to help the single parents broaden their horizons concerning adventures that they as families and individuals can do. Suggest that if they want to do something which someone else has done with their family, that other person might be a good resource for helping them overcome the hurdles they see.

If your group needs a little help thinking of adventures, consider these options:

bowling	visiting museums
tennis	touring and sight-seeing
hiking	trying a new art form
waterskiing	biking
swimming	swap meets
scuba diving	jogging
racquetball	picnics
table games	ball games
fishing	attending dog shows
camping	attending flower shows
classes	mountain climbing
gardening	day trips
carpentry	photography
horseback riding	sailing
visiting relatives	trips to the library

STEP 2

Taking the Risk with the Kids (10 minutes)

Objective: To help single parents review some of the difficult challenges of outlets with their children and share possible solutions.

Share the following:

One of life's hardest tasks is that of deciding to risk. Failure is a very real possibility in every new adventure. But it is well to remember that it is in the possibility of failure that the joy of success is born.

Present the following situations, and ask the class to discuss the risks in each and the possible ways of meeting the challenges. (If the members of your group are able, you might suggest that they try to roleplay these situations.)

● **Going camping for the first time with your three grade-school-age children.**
● **Going to the school open house with your child when you fear that your ex-spouse might be there with his or her new "family."**
● **The grandparents (your ex-spouse's parents) want to come from out of town for their first visit since your separation.**
● **Your nine-year-old son begs you to take him to the baseball game. You've never been to one, and you are sure you won't like it.**

STEP 3

Taking the Risk with Adults (20 minutes)

Objective: To help the class members to identify some of the feelings of insecurity in entering adult social activities as a single. Issues concerning their sexual desires and fears will be discussed.

Discuss the following social situations and their challenges in the same way the previous items relating to the children were discussed. Again, if you are able, have the group try roleplays.

● **Going to your first "single club" outing.**
● **A single man at work is physically very attractive, and you know he finds you attractive. He invites you to his place for a dinner with friends. After the friends leave . . .**
● **You want to go on the weekend retreat with the small group from church, but everyone**

else in the group is married, and you fear that in many activities and discussions you will feel left out.
- A couple has been dating for a year. One person is anxious to marry; the other isn't.

Share the following suggestions and list the title phrases (in italics) on the chalkboard.

1. *Sexual feelings are normal* and a part of being physically human. They do not stop simply because one has become single.

2. *We all have a need to be touched, held, and comforted.* These needs are part of sexual feelings and they are often intensified in periods of emotional stress. Try to plan for alternate ways in which these needs can be at least partially met.

3. *What we see, touch, and hear can arouse sexual feelings.* Try to avoid situations that arouse this energy for which there is no adequate outlet at this time. However, don't become too anxious. Exercise, particularly regular fitness activities, also help.

4. *Sexual feelings are partially emotional intimacy.* Emotional intimacy is the sharing of an experience of deeply felt empathy and concern. Intimacy is the exchange of love when the needs of the other are as important as your needs. It is friendship at its deepest. Try to cultivate one or two friendships at a deep level of intimacy without any physical involvement. Often these will be with another of the same sex. Enjoy these as one of the benefits of singleness.

STEP 4

Moving On Out (10 minutes)

Objective: *To help single parents plan a new social strategy which addresses both activity and intimacy needs.*

Have each class member team up with a partner. Then have the teams talk together about what each person would count as a "perfect day." Have them select from that day one activity that is possible and plan how it can be carried out.

Suggest that team members agree to contact one another at least once during the week—either in person or by phone. The time together should be spent in mutual accountability concerning whether any progress has been made on carrying out their new outlet plan. They can also do further strategy building about new adventures.

Have the team members pray for one another as the session is dismissed.

The Extended Family . . . How Does It Fit?

13

Session Aim: To help single parents utilize the resources of the extended family, the church family, and friends to experience support, counsel, and balanced sex role modeling for the children.

Advance Preparation

In preparation for this session, consider inviting other members of the church who might be interested in supporting single-parent families. Step 4 is designed to foster the creation of an Aid Exchange between single-parent families and others. Other single adults and couples without children in their home might be ideally available and interested in interacting with single-parent families. Read through Step 4 for a further explanation of this idea.

For this session you will also need the following:

1. If you invite additional people for this session because of their interest in and dedication to single parents, you will need extra seating.
2. The class notebook, "Parenting Joys and Struggles."
3. Find and have available for review the transparency, "Servants of Christ" (TR-6), from Session 7. You will also need the transparency, "The Aid Exchange" (TR-10).
4. Copies for everyone of the resource sheets, "Case Studies" (RS-17) and "Ephesians 4—Order and Organization" (RS-18). Make sure that you have extra copies for any extra people who might come if you have invited them.
5. Enough 3" x 5" cards so that everyone in your class and your expected visitors can have about two apiece.
6. A large bulletin board with tacks or stickpins or a wall to which you can safely tape cards.
7. Refreshments to conclude the session and the course. Don't forget to provide extra if you have invited others from the church. This activity will require extra time, but it is highly recommended.

STEP 1

Class Notebook Review (10 minutes)

Objective: To review and offer prayer and praise for the recorded concerns of the single parents.

Welcome other people from the church if they have come, and explain that they are there because of their commitment to and interest in the single-parent families of your church. Mention that later in the session there will be an occasion for seeing how mutual aid can be arranged within the church family.

Direct the attention of the class to the class notebook, "Parenting Joys and Struggles." Review needs which are indicated in the notebook or are added spontaneously by class members. Also, take some time to highlight parenting successes over the quarter. Record new ones. Then spend a period of time in prayer for the continuing needs and in praise for answered prayer.

STEP 2

The Extended Family (20 minutes)

Objective: To help single parents understand the importance of the extended family in meeting emotional, social, physical, and spiritual needs in the single-parent family.

Pass out copies of the resource sheet, "Case Studies" (RS-17), and then divide the class into six groups. Assign each group a different case study.

Ask each group to analyze its case and answer the following questions you will put on the chalkboard:

- **What is happening in this family? What emotional, physical, social, and/or spiritual needs are present?**
- **What would you like to have happen in this family? How can the emotional, physical, social, and/or spiritual needs be filled?**

Allow about ten minutes for analysis and strategy building before asking each small group to report their case and conclusions to the whole class. Whenever possible, ask how the need might be met or eased by other dedicated people in contact with the family.

Use the transparency, "Servants of Christ" (TR-6), to review the *functions* of the family as you lecture the following:

Love and Nurture

No family, whether it is headed by one or two parents, can meet all the needs of its members. Each family is to provide an environment wherein its members, particularly its younger members, can learn to manage relationships. In parent-to-child and child-to-parent interactions, relating is learned across one generation. But think how much richer the experience would be if three or four generations could be regularly spanned.

Think for a moment of your own contact as a child with a favorite grandparent, aunt or uncle. What contributions were made to your life through that relationship?

Allow a few moments for responses from the group, noting their points on the chalkboard.

Cross-generational contacts are extremely important in providing a broad nurture base, various role models, and teaching in a variety of skills (shop, house, yard) and folk wisdom such as child rearing, marital adjustment, and just plain getting on in the world. Older family members extend experience to all of life's developmental issues. The extended family may also provide physical support and assistance at points of stress. For the single parent the need for these gifts is certainly intensified.

On an even broader base, it is well to remember that the church as the local expression of the family of God can provide a family experience to its members—young and old.

Order and Organization

The second family function is related to the socialization of the family members. In this training process family members gain a life-style and value system specific to that particular family. Each family stamps its members with its own brand of order and organization.

And yet, too often in our contemporary society, the isolated nuclear family is expected to shoulder this task alone. But what happens if the prevailing culture is contrary to the family's values and patterns? The children are thrown into tension.

Even in families with two parents, this socialization task becomes nearly impossible if the family is functioning in isolation. How much more important it is for the single-parent family to have the support of an extended family—preferably the biological *and* church family. When this can happen, children don't experience their "oddball" parent against the whole world, but they see two alternative societies. The Christian parent is not left to merely make claims of how much better it is to follow the Lord. Instead, there are a variety of examples of how the Christian way is viable, leads to peace, provides love, and is desirable.

STEP 3

The Treasure of the Church (15 minutes)

Objective: To help single parents explore the potential of the church for being an extended family.

How can the church be an extended family? How can it provide the two functions of love and nurture, and order and organization?

Have the participants turn to I John 4:11-13, and have one person read the passage aloud. Point out that we know God abides in us when we as a local church provide an extended family environment for the members. It is this love and nurture that provides a basis for making disciples.

Distribute copies of the resource sheet, "Ephesians 4—Order and Organization" (RS-18), and have the class turn to Ephesians 4:25-32. Have them note the points of order and organization that are mentioned. This demonstrates the other function of the church that is similar to an extended family.

STEP 4

Enhancing Your Church Family (15 minutes)

Objective: To help the class participants to identify specific ways they could meet each other's needs.

Use the transparency, "The Aid Exchange" (TR-10), covering up the bottom half of the transparency. Ask each participant to list several tasks for which he or she needs help on a sheet of paper using the categories on the need wheel as suggestions.

Then uncover the bottom half of the transparency, and pass out 3" x 5" cards to everyone and suggest that they select one of the needs they have identified on their sheet of paper and write an aid exchange ad for it on the card. Provide extra cards for those who would like to make more than one. Their ads might read like the sample at the bottom of TR-10. The task or need should be specific and the exchange offered specific as well.

This exercise should include those people who aren't single parents since the idea is to get everyone in the church interacting and caring more for one another.

After you have allowed about five minutes for the creation of cards, have as many participants as possible read their cards to the group. When a person reads a card, they should tack it to the bulletin board or tape it to the wall. Later, "takers" can retrieve the cards and make arrangements for the exchange.

Of course, exchanges can be renegotiated from what appears on the cards. Maybe the person willing to fix the screen doors doesn't care much for cherry pies, but could really benefit from having a paper typed. So much the better!

Suggest that this be an ongoing practice in your church either through an active bulletin board or an ad column in your church announcements.

Conclude the course with a time of refreshments and socializing.

Bibliography

Atlas, Stephen. *Single Parenting*. Englewood Cliffs: Prentice-Hall, 1981. This book by a national officer of Parents Without Partners provides a review of strategies that have worked for other single parents as well as himself. The strategies are creative—even invigorating—as the author builds a strong case for the strengths and positive aspects of the single-parent home.

Berman, Eleanor. *The Cooperating Family*. Englewood Cliffs: Prentice-Hall, 1977. Eleanor Berman provides "how to's" in creating family cooperation. All family members are encouraged to take on family responsibility. The book goes beyond ideals, however. Many practical suggestions are offered in implementing a working system of cooperation. Planning is the key strategy. The text provides excellent examples of total family involvement in planning. One such example is in the use of the family meeting which is well illustrated in the book.

Caine, Lynn. *Lifelines*. New York: Doubleday and Company, 1978. Lynn Cain's husband died leaving her a young wife alone with two children. Her first book, *Widow*, offers advice and commentary for others in the event of the death of a spouse. *Lifelines* offers a behind-the-scenes look at single parenting—the tough and devastating as well as the success and victory. This book is biographical. It provides intimate sharing and in that is well worth a reader's time. Single parents will see their own feelings and struggles mirrored in its story.

Guernsey, Dennis. *A New Design for Family Ministry*. Elgin: David C. Cook Publishing Co., 1982. Guernsey, who is the Consulting Editor for this course, argues that churches ought not compete with or drain families, but should instead support family life—single-parent families as well as two-parent families. An invaluable guide for anyone involved in counseling church families.

Klein, Carole. *The Single Parent Experience*. New York: Avon Books, 1973. As the title indicates, this book is wide in its scope. The format is encyclopedic: a number of issues are briefly stated, and then a series of insights and strategies offered. A ready reference book.

Ricci, Isolina. *Mom's House, Dad's House*. New York: MacMillian, 1980. Making shared custody work is easier mandated legally than carried out emotionally and socially in the family broken by divorce or separation. The book is an excellent resource in legal issues and custody law. It covers principles along with practical checklists helpful in moving parents toward a working partnership in their parenting even though such a marital partnership has been broken. Insightful material is provided in the special problems of long-distance parenting. Remarriage concerns are also addressed.

Rosenthal, Kristine and Keshet, Harry. *Fathers Without Partners*. Totowa: Rowman and Littlefield, 1981. Although this book is primarily a sociological study of fathers and their roles after divorce, it provides helpful insights into the emotional and social struggles of the noncustodial parent. An excellent bibliography is included.

Silver, Gerald and Silver, Myra. *Weekend Fathers*. Los Angeles: Stratford Press, 1981. The Silvers provide some well-grounded information on the importance of the father in the single-parent situation. The style of the book provides a readable view of single parenting from the side of the, often, noncustodial father—weekend fathers. A number of practical hints for continuing effective and normalized contact with offspring are outlined.

Jensen, Marilyn. *Formerly Married*. Philadelphia: Westminster Press, 1983. Divorce in the Christian setting is often difficult. Jensen traces her own journey through divorce and single parenting. A number of good suggestions are provided within the format of personal illustration and example. Maintaining family routines is well illustrated.

Johnson, Nancy Karo. *Alone and Beginning Again*. Valley Forge: Judson Press, 1982. Johnson shares her experiences as a young and frightened widow with two preschool children. Learning to cope with competence is the theme.

Reed, Bobbi. *I Didn't Plan to Be a Single Parent*. St. Louis: Concordia Publishing House, 1981. This book provides a comprehensive coverage of single parenting from custody to dating within a Christian perspective. Practical suggestions from other single parents are woven throughout the material.

Smith, Virginia Watts. *The Single Parent*. Old Tappan: Fleming H. Revell Company, 1976. The author shares creative and Scripturally based ideas on single parenting. An excellent development of the crisis or loss cycle is provided. Another topic developed with sensitivity is that of sex and the single Christian.

Course Overview

Negative Labels

Directions: In Column A write down a sticky parenting situation similar to those described by the parents on the tape. In Column B list your most common response to that situation. In Column C put the label you associate with yourself because of your response. In Column D try to identify where you got that label. In Column E list an alternative/better response. In column F put the accompanying positive label.

A Sticky Parenting Situations	B My Response	C Label	D Source	E A Better Response	F New Label
1.					1.
2.					2.
3.					3.
4.					4.
5.					5.
6.					6.

Building Self-Esteem

1. Exploring New Experiences

Let's try it. _____ Don't ask me to change.
       1 2 3 4 5

2. Allowing Time to Change

It takes time. _____ I expect instant change.
       1 2 3 4 5

3. Plan in Small Steps

One step at a time. _____ All or nothing.
       1 2 3 4 5

4. Building Warm, Affirming Friendships

I find friends who do it for me _____ I find friends who tell me how to do it.
       1 2 3 4 5

Behavior Match

Match the following behaviors with the stage in the loss-and-healing cycle by writing in the appropriate stage on the blank: **Denial, Anger/Bargaining, Depression,** or **Acceptance**.

1. _____   John is out every night—classes, dates, overtime at work, etc.

2. _____   Sarah has refused to let anyone touch or remove her husband's clothing and personal items since his death.

3. _____   Each time Bill comes to take the children for an outing, Mary feels a flutter of excitement, half hoping he will stay and talk afterwards.

4. _____   Joan threw Tom's picture in the trash, emphatically verbalizing his every fault all the way to the trash bin and back.

5. _____   Leah has difficulty getting up every morning. Most days she is late for work and the children are late for school. Weekends she stays in bed with the covers pulled over her head.

6. _____   Sandy has gained a great deal of weight in the past months since her divorce. She takes little interest in her clothing and personal grooming.

7. _____   Joe is having difficulty staying on top of things at work. Projects are falling below their usual high quality.

8. _____   Abby has decided to go back to school. Independence and a new career are important new issues in her life.

Finding My Place in the Loss-and-Healing Cycle

Stage	My Typical Behaviors	Healing Helps
Denial		Patient listening Frequent reviewing of the events of loss Understanding and empathy Little pressure to "face reality" Psalm 16: 1, 11
Anger/ Bargaining		Appropriate physical release for anger A "sounding board" to listen Little pressure to calm down Psalm 94
Depression		Maintain regular routines and exercise Free expression of grief and mourning Emotional release Counseling Psalm 30
Acceptance		New goals and outlets Assistance with refocusing plans Physical and emotional outlets Psalm 118

Self-Growth Contract

List your three top priorities in terms of your family:

1. _____

2. _____

3. _____

Consider the following areas of your life and try to state what goals you have. In the right column identify any obstacles and potential solutions for overcoming those obstacles.

	Goals	*Obstacles/Solutions*
Spiritual Job/Career Physical Social Management Income Homemaking Maintenance		

Select one of the areas mentioned above, the one you think is most immediately attainable. Fill in the following contract in terms of that goal.

I, _____, have decided to increase my competence in _____, by

working toward the specific goal of being able to _____. The

first step I must take to accomplish this is to identify my present way of functioning in this area. It could be

specifically described as: _____.

_____

In a similar situation I hope to be able to _____

_____.

I will begin to develop this new competence by _____

_____.

I will know some progress has been made when I can observe that I _____

_____,

and I will report that progress to my partner, _____.

Signed, _____ Date: _____

Signed, _____ Date: _____
(Growth partner)

Loss Roleplays

A. Michael is 15 months old. His mother is in the hospital. His father is always in a hurry to return to the hospital or return to work. He has little time for the youngster. The baby-sitter is loving but Michael seems withdrawn. He sits with a sad expression and is difficult to draw into play. He is not interested in eating but is passive in his resistance to mealtimes. He is not passive at bedtimes, though. He resists vigorously—screaming and crying. This seems to be the only time of day that he has any energy.

B. Mario, age eight, covered his ears when his mother and father told him of their plans to get a divorce. Later in the week he comes home from play and calls out in the house, "Dad, Dad, are you home? Can we play ball?" Even though he knows his dad has moved out, he keeps his ball, mitt, and bat beside the front door ready for Dad to come home.

C. Sarah is ten years old. She is happy that her mother left the family. "Now all that nagging and yelling is gone to," she reminds anyone who will listen. One afternoon when Sarah is home alone she throws out all of her mother's things. When the rest of the family returns home, Sarah has prepared supper and made a cake.

D. Billy is always fidgeting, squirming, bumping, giggling, and talking. His conversations are difficult to follow since his train of thought is not always clear. It almost seems that his object is just to talk not to actually communicate ideas. Frenzy is the best way to describe his activity level.

E. Jeff is resistant to any suggestion. He often clearly does the opposite of what he is asked both at home and at school. Since his father left, he seems angry and in fact has gotten into a number of fights.

F. Mary is six and recently adopted by a very loving family, but nothing pleases her. She cries and moans at any slight, real or imagined. "I fell," "He looked at me," "It's my turn to sit by the window," all trigger a flood of tears.

G. Jason is always smiling. He seems eager to please, but then nothing ever gets done. That is, nothing ever gets done on the good days. On the bad days, Jason often breaks or messes things up in his efforts to please and do what he's told. On the worst days, Jason may do something like vomit all over the meal table just as the baby-sitter arrives so that his mother can go out for the evening.

Responses to Loss

Below are listed some of the common symptoms for the three stages of children's response to loss.

Protest	Anger	Hope
Passive responses	Resistance	Good-byes
Difficult bedtimes	Fighting	Hellos
Denial	Mourning	
Yearning/searching	Perfect behavior	
Rejecting	Accidents	
Hyperactivity	Physical symptoms	
Disorganization		

On the left list your children's names (use extra paper if necessary). Then under each of the three headings identify the behaviors you currently observe. Finally, fill in how you can help.

	Protest	Anger	Hope
Name: _____ I can help by . . .			
Name: _____ I can help by . . .			

What Is the Function?

Look up the Scriptures assigned to you and write down a key word or summary word of the family function that is mentioned. Then check off whether it is a love-and-nurture function or an order-and-organization function.

	Key/Summary Word	Love and Nurture	Order and Organization
Proverbs 1: 8, 9			
Proverbs 4: 1-4			
Exodus 20: 12			
Deuteronomy 6: 1-7			
Ephesians 6: 1-4			
Psalm 103: 13			
Psalm 68: 3-6			
Deuteronomy 24: 5			
I Peter 3: 1-8			
Colossians 3: 18-21			
Psalm 101: 1, 2			
I John 4: 11, 12			

Your Energy Bank

On this list of responsibilities and activities, check off the impact each one has on your energy level. Mark *both* what each one takes out of you *and* what it provides. The scales are from zero to three, with three being the most draining or invigorating, respectively.

	"How much it takes out of me." Debit (−)				"How much I get out of doing it." (+) Credit			
	3	2	1	0	0	1	2	3
Earning a living								
Playing with the children								
Helping with homework								
Having daily prayer								
Maintaining the car								
Doing the shopping								
Going to church								
Cooking								
Setting rules								
Enforcing rules								
Leading family devotions								
Taking a night out with friends								
Reading (newspaper, magazine, or novel)								
Doing home maintenance								
Transporting the children to activities								
Keeping an even temper								
Being strong and stable for the kids								
Settling fights								
Reading to the family								
Hugging and cuddling kids								
Managing the budget								
Exercising regularly								
Making major purchases								
Subtotals of each column				0	0			
Energy balance	−				+			

To obtain the subtotals, count the number of checks in each column and multiply by the value of the column. The zero columns are, of course, zero.

To obtain your energy balance, add the totals of the debit columns to give you a measure of your energy drain. Then compare that to the total of your credit columns to see whether you are in the red or black.

Don't be too surprised by the score. This is not a precise tool, but use it to stimulate your thinking about whether you are trying to be a superparent.

Building Trust Bonds

Select one or more responses which you feel will strengthen the trust bond between parent and child in the following situations.

1. Billy, age ten, is a strong defender of his father even though his dad appears late or not at all for visitation times. Billy's frustrated mother should . . .
   a. Tell Billy she doesn't want to hear anymore about his father.
   b. Try to make Billy's father understand how disappointing his inconsistency is to Billy.
   c. Allow Billy to work out his own relationship with his dad.

2. Joanie leaves her bike unlocked on the front porch although she has been warned not to do so. The day before the bike hike with the junior high youth group, the bike is stolen. Joanie's mother should . . .
   a. Give Joanie a loan to buy a new bike.
   b. Sympathize with Joanie concerning her loss.
   c. Suggest that Joanie rent or borrow a bike for the trip.
   d. Tell Joanie it is her fault, and she'll have to save to get a bike for herself.

3. Three-year-old Mary is afraid of the dark. She often refuses to go to bed. Her father is having a difficult time coping with this new fear. She was such a confident child before her mother left. He should . . .
   a. Purchase a night-light and sit quietly on the bed for a few minutes after good-night prayers.
   b. Take care to establish a consistent bedtime routine.
   c. Encourage Mary to talk about the loss of her mother.
   d. Insist that Mary go to bed and stop making such a fuss.
   e. Have Mary call her mother each night before bedtime.

4. Robert's mother would like him to sleep through the night now that he is 20 months. But he has recently been waking up more often—five or six times a night—demanding to get up and eat and wailing when he can't. His mother should . . .
   a. Get some earplugs, close the doors, and ignore him.
   b. Feed him as he pleases, hoping he will grow out of the stage.
   c. Go to him to assure him of her presence, maybe putting him back down and patting his back, but refusing to get him up or feed him.
   d. Call his father and tell him that Robert is entering the terrible twos early and she can't cope.

5. Timmy, age four, wants to go to the park by himself. It is two blocks away and safe, but Timmy is not careful crossing streets. She should . . .
   a. Tell him he can't go unless she goes with him.
   b. Let him go, and pray that he will be safe.
   c. Tell Timmy he can go when he learns how to cross streets safely. Then, tell him he can show her how much he knows by walking with her, watching out for her, and telling her what should happen at each corner.

6. Laurie is 17 and works each day after school. She wants to eat at McDonald's and go straight to the library to study with friends until 10 p.m. before coming home each night. Her mother should . . .
   a. Allow this as a step in granting her freedom.
   b. Insist that she have her meal at home for the sake of the life of the whole family, but then allow her to study at the library as long as her grades remain up.
   c. Compromise and permit Laurie's plan two nights per week.
   d. Refuse to go along with the plan because Laurie is not yet an adult and ready to live on her own.

Stages and Tasks

Identify the tasks in the areas of the physical, social, cognitive (knowledge), and emotional according to each state. Begin with the age of your oldest child. Then fill in the other stages later. See the adult stage for an example of the kinds of tasks to include.

Infant Goal: Trust

To develop security through physical comfort as physical needs are met in predictable patterns.

Physical   Social   Cognitive   Emotional

Toddler Goal: Autonomy

To develop an I-can-do-it-myself confidence through increased mastery of physical skills.

Physical   Social   Cognitive   Emotional

Pre-School Goal: Initiative

To develop an increased sense of separateness through making independent choices and initiating activities based on personal preference.

Physical   Social   Cognitive   Emotional

Stages and Tasks (cont'd.)

School-Age Goal: Industry

To develop the special skills and talents which increase competence at home, at school, at church, and in the neighborhood.

Physical	Social	Cognitive	Emotional

Adolescent Goal: Identity

To develop an integrated and independent sense of self, separate from family but related to friends.

Physical	Social	Cognitive	Emotional

Adult Goal: Intimacy

To develop skills in sharing oneself in deep relationships. To learn to give, care, share, and sacrifice for others.

Physical	*Social*	*Cognitive*	*Emotional*
Adequate exercise and diet.	Build support systems.	Continue growth through new interests and demands.	Manage life transitions.
Manage sexual issues.	Choose/develop marriage or singleness.		Learn to accept loss.
Recreational interests.	Build a family.		Learn to manage stress.
	Enter into church and community.		

Next Steps

1. Child's name: _____ 2. Developmental stage: _____

3. List any tasks the child has basically mastered in this stage _____

   _____

4. Identify one task which is yet to be mastered. Select one for which you think

   the child is ready. _____

5. On the scales below try to evaluate how difficult this task will be for your child
   to master based on that child's four life perspectives.

	1	2	3	4	5
Introversion/Extroversion	hard				easy
Thinking/Feeling	1	2	3	4	5
Mechanical/Verbal	1	2	3	4	5
Closed/Open	1	2	3	4	5

6. Given the above evaluation, what one small step do you think would be the
   next appropriate step you could initiate to help your child master his or her
   new task?

   _____

7. What will you need to do this next week to get things underway?

   _____

Real Men / Women Don't . . .

Recently a couple books spoofed stereotyped sex roles. Here you can do the same by listing some of the things commonly thought uncharacteristic of *real* men or *real* women. Follow the style of the titles in making your lists.

1. Real Men Don't Eat Quiche

2.

3.

1. Real Women Don't Pump Gas

2.

3.

What I Can Do Best

Child's name	In terms of sexual identity, I can help . . .	A person of the opposite sex is needed to help	Possible candidates

Case Studies

1. Mary is the sole support of two young children. She works in an office at an occupation she does not enjoy, but it is the only one for which she has skills. Each month by the time she pays child care, rent, food, and a few other bills she is broke.

2. Steven, age seven and the youngest of three children, is very interested in his 14-year-old sister's nail polish, hair curlers, and pretty dresses. He also plays with her discarded Barbie dolls. Steven's mother and father are divorced, although he does have some limited contact with his dad. Douglas, the oldest child at 16, has a hard time relating positively to his younger brother.

3. Ryan, age eight, is having difficulty in school. Not only is his behavior inappropriate, but his learning is slow. He has difficulty concentrating and is not interested in learning. His mother JoAnn is discouraged and has a lot of trouble helping him at home as the teacher has suggested. She begins okay, but soon loses patience. Yelling, nagging, and lecturing begin. As much as possible JoAnn avoids the teacher. That way she doesn't have to hear about and get discouraged over Ryan.

4. Emily is furious with Sam. His child support payments are always late and insufficient. She is living on less than half their previous income but is having increasing trouble meeting basic expenses. She is making it harder for Sam to see the children because she doesn't think he deserves to see them. In response he is more and more reluctant to pay his share of the child support.

5. Sarah is having a great deal of difficulty adjusting to the death of her husband. Also, James, her oldest at 19, has decided to drop out of college to "experience life." Sarah is beside herself with concern and worry. She feels unable to cope with Jame's decision. She is also afraid that Tom, age 17, is experimenting with drugs and alcohol. He, too, seems to have no direction. Sarah feels that the lack of a strong male figure is taking its toll.

6. Jessica is young and unmarried and the mother of a preemie. The infant is now at home but needs constant care and watching. The baby needs to be fed every two hours and should be participating in an infant stimulation program. Jessica is on welfare and has not yet finished high school. She is feeling far from loving toward the infant. Anger, frustration, and isolation are her dominant feelings.

Ephesians 4—Order and Organization

Note the ways mentioned in Ephesians 4: 25-32 that the church is to fulfill the family function of encouraging order and organization between people in the church.

Verse	Task	Function
25	Speak truthfully	Enhances order
26	In your anger do not sin	Preserves order
26	Make peace quickly	Restores order
28	Do not steal	Creates order
28	Work in order to share	Develops caring organization
29	Avoid unwholesome talk	Preserves order
29	Say what is helpful	Enhances organization
31	Get rid of bitterness, etc.	Protects order
32	Promote kindness and forgiveness	Such organization extends Christ's love